Critical Fictions

Nerval's 'Les Illuminés'

THE EUROPEAN HUMANITIES RESEARCH CENTRE

UNIVERSITY OF OXFORD

The European Humanities Research Centre of the University of Oxford organizes a range of academic activities, including conferences and workshops, and publishes scholarly works under its own imprint, LEGENDA. Within Oxford, the EHRC bridges, at the research level, the main humanities faculties: Modern Languages, English, Modern History, Literae Humaniores, Music and Theology. The Centre stimulates interdisciplinary research collaboration throughout these subject areas and provides an Oxford base for advanced researchers in the humanities.

The Centre's publications programme focuses on making available the results of advanced research in medieval and modern languages and related interdisciplinary areas. An Editorial Board, whose members are drawn from across the British university system, covers the principal European languages. Titles include works on French, German, Italian, Portuguese, Russian and Spanish literature. In addition, the EHRC co-publishes with the Society for French Studies, the British Comparative Literature Association and the Modern Humanities Research Association. The Centre also publishes *Oxford German Studies* and has launched a Special Lecture Series under the LEGENDA imprint.

Enquiries about the Centre's publishing activities should be addressed to:
Professor Malcolm Bowie, Director

Further information:
Kareni Bannister, Senior Publications Officer
European Humanities Research Centre
47 Wellington Square, Oxford OX1 2JF
enquiries@ehrc.ox.ac.uk
www.ehrc.ox.ac.uk

LEGENDA

RESEARCH MONOGRAPHS IN FRENCH STUDIES

LEGENDA

European Humanities Research Centre
Research Monographs in French Studies 3

Critical Fictions
Nerval's *Les Illuminés*

❖

Meryl Tyers

LEGENDA

European Humanities Research Centre
University of Oxford
Research Monographs in French Studies 3
1998

Published for the Society for French Studies by the
European Humanities Research Centre
of the University of Oxford
47 Wellington Square
Oxford OX1 2JF

LEGENDA is the publications imprint of the
European Humanities Research Centre

ISBN 1 900755 15 7

First published 1998

British Library Cataloguing in Publication Data
A CIP catalogue record for this book is available from the British Library

LEGENDA series designed by Cox Design Partnership, Witney, Oxon
Printed in Great Britain by
Information Press
Eynsham
Oxford OX18 1JJ

CONTENTS

To the memory of my maternal grandparents
George Frederick William Adams, 1902–89
and
Louisa Beatrice Maud Adams, 1906–94

PREFACE

'No significant study', wrote James Villas in 1968, 'has yet been devoted to *Les Illuminés*, an extremely complex work that leads the reader into Nerval's strange esoteric world and that illustrates further the poet's narrative technique.' And this observation holds largely true three decades on. One of the obstacles to a fuller understanding of this text is that it is seldom studied in its own right, and frequently included in more general schemes whose focus is elsewhere. The purpose of this book, therefore, is to draw together disparate facts, references, evaluations and commentary on the writings that make up *Les Illuminés* so that they build into a picture that is complete and, I hope, useful.

The publication, between 1984 and 1993, of an entirely new scholarly edition of Nerval's *Œuvres complètes*, edited by Jean Guillaume and Claude Pichois in the Pléiade series, was a significant step forward, so that it became possible to view much of Nerval's writing in a fresh light, and this study should, therefore, be read in the context of the new Pléiade text of *Les Illuminés* and the critical apparatus relating to it. Max Milner's essays, both there (as section-editor) and in his pre-existent Folio edition of the text (1976), are richly imaginative and suggestive, and they certainly serve as the best serious introductions to reading *Les Illuminés*.

However, an edition necessarily has limited scope for surveying the detail of critical discourse, or for close study showing, for instance, how pertinent the contemporary circumstances of *Les Illuminés* might prove to an understanding of Nerval's intentions and of his attitude towards his book: it would be difficult to prove or disprove that these intentions were significant without having first acquired some framework of reference concerning them. The present largely factual study is able to address these issues and others, and seeks to encourage further readings and interpretations, hoping to create a real reappraisal of an exciting and complex book. The six constituent biographical sketches and their preface, 'La Bibliothèque de mon oncle', are not purely fragmentary, and here I have sought to gather together information relevant to the whole book, and to take into account the experience of reading it *as* a whole.

Meryl Tyers
Glasgow, 1998

ACKNOWLEDGEMENTS

I should like to thank Max Milner, who encouraged my original project of studying the poetic possibilities of *Les Illuminés* at a turning point in my research; his critical work on *Les Illuminés* inspired me. I am very grateful to Alan Raitt, Michael Sheringham, Alison Finch, Ceri Crossley and Michael Moriarty for their objective comments at various stages.

While doing the research for this project, I taught and studied at Fitzwilliam College, Cambridge, the Ecole Normale Supérieure, and St Anne's College, Oxford, on a postdoctoral fellowship, and did revisions during a period of sabbatical leave supported by grants from the British Academy and Glasgow University: my heartfelt thanks for their teaching and friendship to those in all four places including Judith Angell, Katie Attwood, Colin Davis, Lisa Davis, Rhiannon Goldthorpe, Rachael Langford, Catherine Léglu, Rosemary Lloyd, David Martin, Laura Martin, Graham Nelson, Jim Simpson, Finn Sinclair and Emma Wilson. My greatest debts of gratitude are to Robert Lethbridge, and to Peter Collier; it is a particular pleasure to be able to thank them for their long-term encouragements here.

ABBREVIATIONS AND CONVENTIONS

NPl 1, *NPl 2*, *NPl 3* (*Nouvelle Pléiade*)—Gérard de Nerval, *Œuvres complètes*, edited by Jean Guillaume and Claude Pichois.

APl 1, *APl 2* (*Ancienne Pléiade*)—Gérard de Nerval, *Œuvres*, edited by Albert Béguin and Jean Richer (first edition).

'Lecou edition'—First edition of *Les Illuminés* (Paris: Victor Lecou, 1852).

Full publication details are to be found in the Bibliography. The first edition of Béguin and Richer's Pléiade is used because it is the most widely available: discussions of differences amongst editions are fully referenced in notes.

All citations are given in the form of a first footnote with subsequent citations appearing in parentheses directly after each extract. Individual story titles from *Les Illuminés* are given inside quotation marks, as representing parts of the larger volume. In extracts, italics are copied from the source, unless otherwise indicated.

'Je demande que l'on respecte l'édition en quatre volumes du *Perceforest*,—un héros d'autrefois ...; édition unique, avec deux pages transposées et une énorme tache d'encre au troisième volume.'

...

'Le *Perceforest* incomplet! Les révolutions sont épouvantables!'

Les Faux Saulniers

CHAPTER 1

Texts and Contexts

Introduction

The title *Les Illuminés* is allusive—but hardly enlightening. Initially, it may suggest an eighteenth-century sect, special personalities, and a mysterious symbolism connected with light. Somewhere, nevertheless, between the restrictive dictionary definitions of *Illuminati* and the abstract concept of illumination, one can locate a matrix of factual information, fictional construction and meaningful indeterminacy, in the shape of this series of biographies which constantly defy both categorization and synthesis. In the French language, it is not Gérard de Nerval but Rimbaud who is credited with having revived the use, current in English but obscure in the French of his contemporaries, of *illumination* to mean a colourful coverage of margins using illustration; in the French lexicon, this semantic gap had for centuries been filled by the word *enluminure*, and since the sixteenth century *illumination* had not been used. In Littré's definition of *illuminer*, under 'Historique du mot', the following sixteenth-century example is given from La Boétie: 'Les petits enfans qui, pour voir les luisans images de livres illuminez, apprennent à lire'.[1] Yet, in defiance of linguistic diachrony (Rimbaud was three months old when Nerval died), *Les Illuminés* are indeed metaphorically illuminations—they use the medium of narrative in an illustrative treatment of marginal figures.

The attitude taken in many critiques of *Les Illuminés*, overtly or not, is that this work represents a series of marginalia in comparison with Nerval's more characteristic and poetic work; the individual pieces are picturesque illuminations which are held to refer us inexorably to some more significant part of the Nervalian page. For readers familiar with the other mature Nervalian texts—the multi-layered temporal

[1] Littré (1963), IV, 738–9.

structures of *Sylvie* and the other *Filles du Feu*, the hermetic symbolism of *Les Chimères* or the tantalizing visions of *Aurélia*—*Les Illuminés* may perhaps seem peripheral. Its style is heterogeneous, its themes eclectic, and one has to work to recognize the luminous and characteristic brilliance which draws Nerval's work into the sights of so much scholarly enquiry. More problematically still, it is questionable whether *Les Illuminés* offers a prototype for that elusive definitive text and heroic enterprise, the Nervalian autobiography.[2] But I would argue that, far from being the end of the story, these features are just the beginning of an interpretative quest. What we have here is not an arbitrary agglomeration, but a text which, as well as a collection of individual prose pieces, can be read as a singular, intra-textually patterned entity.

There is a need to redress the balance in favour of a text which repays closer attention, especially when read as a nexus of individual prose pieces whose whole is more than the simple sum of its parts. Its parts vary in style and focus, but those who know the complex relationships into which one must delve to make sense of Nerval's work and its textual histories will be familiar with the sense of a cluster or network of writings constantly rearranged in the imagination and on the page, whose every published form, such as the one with which we shall be dealing here, could be considered a snapshot, one frame in the flow of a reel of film.

In the light of the need for a reassessment of extant material, along with the possibility of a justifiably different reading of *Les Illuminés*, my aims here are broadly twofold. The first is to discern and delineate the significance of *Les Illuminés* in the range of Nerval's total output. This significance is partly defined by the perspectives of Nerval and of his time. The development of French literature over a twelve-year period can be traced in the lineaments of *Les Illuminés*: its first study, 'Le Roi de Bicêtre', dates from 1839, just past the height of the Romantic movement in France, and the last from 1852, in the period of artistic disillusionment and intellectual alienation following the *coup d'état* and the renewal of strict censorship. Its significance can also be defined by the horizons of current scholarly attitudes to *Les Illuminés*, at the point to which these attitudes have evolved over the course of the twentieth century—a century whose radical reinterpretation of

[2] See Michel Jeanneret, 'Nerval et la biographie impossible', *French Studies* 24 (1970), 127–43.

Nerval's importance began with the enlightened intervention of Proust. The assessment of perspectives 'external' to the work is grounded, of course, in the conventions of fact and of history. But comparing the history *Les Illuminés* overtly traces with its blurring of many of the factual markers of that same history is only one critical option. My second aim is to foster a critical reading of this text as something other than a flawed collection of unreliable biographical documents. An adequate reading of the poetically significant content, as opposed to merely the factual documentation and inexactitude, of the whole work is necessary to our understanding of this transition phase in the author's career.

In examining *Les Illuminés* as a text with polyvalent interpretative possibilities, I do not attempt exhaustive comparisons with Nerval's sources, or diverge at length into discussion of much-investigated mystical and Masonic themes which have already received critical attention, although I briefly cover the historical basis of Illuminism, which is important to understanding Nerval's very individual inflection of the subject in *Les Illuminés*. There is no lack of learned comment on the occult and the esoterically symbolic in Nerval's writing, nor on the 'portes d'ivoire ou de corne' which separate Nerval's consciousness of time and of history from more conventional ones. *Les Illuminés* can always be made to fit with ease into thematic studies on these areas of interest because of its subject. The work of Jean Richer, of course, epitomizes the extensive exploration of critical avenues linked to Freemasonry and mysticism: he underlines the significance of *Les Illuminés* ('La lecture des *Illuminés* demeure, croyons-nous, indispensable à qui veut prendre une vue complète de la biographie intellectuelle de l'écrivain,' *APl 2*, xii), but for reasons which differ substantially from those proposed here: 'Elle [la lecture du texte] ne peut que faciliter la pénétration du reste de son œuvre et, singulièrement, des *Chimères*. Et, en elle-même, la biographie de Jacques Cazotte mérite de prendre place parmi les meilleurs récits de Gérard'. This is a combination of reference outward to a text seen as more central and a personal opinion which is by no means a majority view of 'Jacques Cazotte'. But research into mysticism and (often contentious) Masonic linkages in no way exhausts the possibilities opened up by the thematics of this text.

The assertion that *Les Illuminés* has been wrongly viewed as a marginal text or a series of 'unusable' fragments might be countered by the comment that it has not often been the object of *exclusive* critical attention because of the transparent importance of its themes to central Nervalian preoccupations, so that it calls up immediate and unavoidable references to its Nervalian intertexts, as it does for Richer, in my previous example. However, even a quite simple test, quantifying the frequency with which articles referring principally to *Les Illuminés* occur, soon reveals the lesser degree of attention accorded to it, compared, for example, with *Les Filles du Feu* or *Le Voyage en Orient*, two other major texts which take the form of compilations. A search, using the entire run of the *Cahiers Gérard de Nerval* and based both on titles of articles and on titles occurring in the 'Bibliographie' and 'Livres reçus' sections (excluding translations), yields the following proportions of items on the most well-known texts:

Les Filles du Feu or its elements	58
(of which items on *Sylvie*	33)
Aurélia	56
Le Voyage en Orient	34
Les Chimères	34
Les Illuminés	16
(of which items on one piece in isolation	10)

The *Cahiers* do not provide an exhaustive record by any means, but this dedicated journal was one of only two such, representing a major strand of opinion in Nerval studies at their time of publication, and the amounts of attention accorded to the respective texts are a fair guide to the proportions found elsewhere.[3]

Three different strategies are brought into play in this study: textual history, critical discourse (contemporary and modern) and finally a move towards new readings. This first chapter looks at the relevant conditions in which Nerval decided to publish his book, what it represented in his writing career and what it meant or did not mean in relation to his political stance at the time, particularly in the context of one of its two subtitles. Each narrative that makes up *Les Illuminés* is briefly commented upon. Reassessing some of the letters written just after the recently revised publication date of this text has led me

[3] The intermittent series, *Etudes nervaliennes et romantiques*, represents another strand, but is less useful for this type of assessment, as its overt intent is to publish the results of mainly documentary research carried out during the preparation of the *Nouvelle Pléiade* volumes, and the quantity of articles published is determined by the amount of factual adjustment or gap-filling required in the case of specific texts, rather than by simple critical interest. The *Cahiers* are themed, but not rigidly so.

to reviews of it not indicated in the *Nouvelle Pléiade* edition. Nerval's attempts to obtain reviews of his new book, reflected in letters, are an indication of his attitude towards his writing at this time, as is the fact of combining previously published pieces such as these in one volume. Contemporary reviews are discussed: they shed light on literary preoccupations of the time as well as providing an understanding of the implications the book would be deemed to have by a contemporary readership. Chapter 2 surveys the editions of *Les Illuminés* and critical commentaries focusing on the whole text. Studies of individual sections of the work cannot be overlooked, although they fragment what I read as a single work; yet, as an assemblage of disparate information their insights remain valuable especially where they unintentionally illuminate an aspect which runs through the collection. My survey of related scholarship thus relies on the distinction already drawn between two opposing ways of looking at *Les Illuminés*: studies which comment on a single constituent part, and which can often make this depend entirely for its significance on associations with Nerval's other work or with his own biography, are treated after those, less numerous, which treat the book as a whole. The possibilities for linking *Les Illuminés* with other pieces of writing are endless: they are and have been regularly exploited. Such links as have been made must of course be taken into account, but there is an equal need to draw out and discuss its many intra-textual resonances. I argue that the text should be treated both as singular (it is a collection whose publication the author supervised and for which he wrote a prefatory statement) and as plural (these texts are heterogeneous narratives first published at different times and in diverse journals).

Factual contextualization and thematic interpretation eventually converge. Nerval's interest in the (paradoxically) mystical rationalism of the eighteenth century is considered, and what may be meant or implied by his own use of the semantic field of Illuminism. The use of the word *illuminés* is informed by the small number of unequivocal definitions which can be found of the historical term, but Nerval's implied and actual use of the term nevertheless personalizes these definitions, while his use of the related semantic field of illumination has affected its subsequent definitions as much as Rimbaud's use of the same term. Attention shifts towards the meaning of illumination in its general senses, against a background of the imaginary library, and the whole becomes fundamental to the architectonics of the text's cohesiveness. Some of the more prominent pre-texts and intertexts that can be identified are discussed. The final two chapters use images of private libraries and clandestine reading(s), as suggested by the themes of 'La Bibliothèque de mon oncle'. By the end, therefore, the imaginatively involved reader or readers in the focus are present-day, rather than nineteenth-century, ones. The concluding emphasis is on finding a new response suited to modern readers of the Nervalian text, set against responses to other writings. *Les Illuminés* could be argued to be as innovative and suggestive as Nerval's later prose, yet even if we remain sceptical on this point, it is traversed by passages of the prose style that is to come, and it certainly marks a crossroads in the development of later Nervalian writing.

Les Illuminés is diverse, diffuse but nevertheless cohesive, with aid from its ambiguous preface. To the extent that it is possible to speak of (or imply) 'self-coherence' in any Nervalian text, it is possible to say it of *Les Illuminés*. One way of identifying the 'self-cohesive' approach might be to call it structuralist-inspired. If so, then since it is possible to speak of an *Analyse structurale des 'Chimères'*, as Jacques Geninasca does, despite their many outwardly referring elements, it should be possible to do so for *Les Illuminés*.[4] However, there is no deliberate intent to follow a structuralist analysis here, or any prescription other than that of identifying the need for new readings, and suggesting ways in which these could usefully be approached.

Interpreting a text as perceptibly unified and self-indicating may incline one's reading to highlight a certain amount of textual narcissism: but this is a valid counterbalance to the 'self-blindness' fostered by the opposite, centrifugal type of reading. Referring to his own selected corpus of Nerval's writings in *La Lettre perdue*, Michel Jeanneret seems to imply that all synthesizing tendencies in criticism are questionable: 'Les récits interrogés ici constituent chacun un ensemble autonome, porteur d'un sens propre et susceptible d'instaurer, entre écriture et folie, une économie spécifique. On ne cherchera pas à les réduire à une œuvre unique, ni à leur demander une réponse globale'. If his book is in the form of a series of independent essays, this is because of the nature of his subject, 'au nom de l'irréductible singularité de toute réalisation littéraire'.[5] As far

[4] Neuchâtel: La Baconnière, 1971.

[5] *La Lettre perdue: écriture et folie dans l'œuvre de Nerval* (Paris: Flammarion, 1978), 12.

as *Les Illuminés* is concerned, however, reductivity consists of over-selectivity, symptomatic perhaps of an inability to discern the 'économie spécifique' of the entire collected work; and the present reading does not seek a universal fixity, but a 'sens propre', capable, once traced, of greater complexity and infinite modification.

What might *Les Illuminés* yield as a linguistic object, a series of patterns, as a commentary upon itself, and thus as a literary landmark on its own, to which other writings might in turn be compared? What, in other words, is its literary, and its Nervalian, individuality? The following chapters seek to collate a significant, although selective, mass of information, some of which is new, and all of which is brought together expressly to enable these answers at least to be sought in one place.

Nerval's Writing and Politics in 1852

Les Illuminés was published in the early days of May 1852: 'le *Feuilleton du Journal de la Librairie* [du 8 mai] mentionne *Les Illuminés* parmi les "nouvelles publications" de l'éditeur Victor Lecou. Prix: 3,50F; net: 2,40. On a ainsi à quelques jours près (le feuilleton est hebdomadaire) la date de mise en vente du livre'.[6] At the time, Nerval was away in Belgium or Holland, having left in what Gautier described as 'un état de cervelle assez peu rassurant mais guéri physiquement du moins en apparence';[7] the late spring trip followed a winter in which a play he had co-written had flopped, despite initial enthusiasm, causing him mental and physical illness from which he had taken some time to recover. On his journey, Nerval met up with Dumas and his secretary in Brussels, visited the Rijksmuseum and donated an autographed copy of *L'Imagier de Harlem*, the play of the previous winter, to the royal library in The Hague. The precise date of his return to Paris is not known, but he was back by 1 June.

Les Illuminés was subtitled *Récits et portraits* on the title page, but *Les Précurseurs du socialisme* on the front cover, and there is no indication which of these, if either, the author favoured. It contained six

[6] Jean Guillaume and Claude Pichois, 'Chronologie de sa vie et de son œuvre, août 1850–juin 1852', *Etudes nervaliennes et romantiques* 6 (1984), 45. This is an expanded version of the Chronology in *NPl 2*. Until it was rectified in 1984, the publication date had always been given as November (six months later), because the volume was only recorded in the *Bibliographie de la France* on the 20th of that month.

[7] Letter to Ernesta Grisi, 7 May 1852.

biographical sketches, which were fictional to varying extents and had all appeared before in more ephemeral publications: 'Le Roi de Bicêtre', 'Histoire de l'abbé de Bucquoy', 'Les Confidences de Nicolas', 'Jacques Cazotte', 'Cagliostro' and 'Quintus Aucler'. These were accompanied by a remarkable, if succinct, preface, 'La Bibliothèque de mon oncle', which had been newly written.

The 44-year-old Nerval's career at precisely this time was undergoing a transformation. He had begun reorganizing material, collating it into larger units, and had started to identify those of his works which he hoped would be worthy of lasting esteem. He had from early days edited anthologies of others' writing, adding his own prefaces which give crucial clues to his literary attitudes (see *Les Poésies allemandes* (1829) and *Introduction au Choix de poésies de Ronsard* (1830)), and had published his own poems, plays and of course translations from the German, notably *Faust*. Some attribute Nerval's now increasingly serious treatment of his own writing to the fact that he had only lately learned of Goethe's high opinion of his translation of the first *Faust* in 1826, when he was not yet 20. He had started his publishing career early, then, and by now was more than accustomed to seeing his name in print, but a vast amount of his output had been in the underestimated form of theatrical reviews and chronicles describing contemporary cultural events and personalities, appearing in a variety of newspapers.[8]

Following the chronological arrangement of the *Nouvelle Pléiade*, it is possible to pick out the first appearances of fictional narrative in Nerval's career: arguably, the very first is his apparent 'translation' of Jean-Paul Richter's *Le Bonheur de la maison*, which he in fact wrote himself.[9] It is less easy, though, to identify the first examples of imaginative prose exclusively by Nerval to appear inside the covers of a book. Book publication is a criterion more valid currently than it would have been in the nineteenth-century context of serialized or periodical forms of first publication; and it is equally problematic to talk of writing *exclusively* by Nerval, because of his well-documented borrowings from intermediary texts alongside the avowed primary sources (witness his transcriptions from various sources for his travel impressions in *Le Voyage en Orient*). But, caveats aside, it is with the

[8] See *NPl 1*, and Michel Brix's detailed scholarship there and in 'Nerval journaliste', *Etudes nervaliennes et romantiques* 8 (1986).

[9] *Mercure de France* (30 Apr. 1831); *NPl 1*, 314–18.

appearance of *Scènes de la vie orientale*, appearing in two substantial parts, that Nerval's work began its decisive moves away from the world of slighter publications in 1848–50.[10] There was a *tirage à part* of the serialized 'Nuits du Ramazan' taken from *Le National* in mid-1850. The Charpentier edition of *Le Voyage en Orient*, the definitive volume of the travel writings, followed in 1851.

Thus, appearing in 1852, *Les Illuminés* was still one of Nerval's first true books, and only the third collection of his mature work. From this as from many other points of view, it represents a telling choice of material. Before examining the different elements of its history of publication (manuscripts, editions etc.), one of the subtitles, 'Précurseurs du socialisme', calls for a brief look at evidence of Nerval's political attitude in 1852 and whether his attitude to socialism is to be an overriding factor in the context of *Les Illuminés*.

There are reasons why one might expect some form of political stance to be at least detectable. The young Nerval had shared with many of his generation a yearning for the lost glories of France in the Napoleonic era, which he had been too young to experience directly: it seems not implausible that the figure of Louis-Napoléon (soon to become Napoléon III) should, at least initially, have held some attraction for him. But it is equally plausible that closer acquaintance should have worked to the detriment of Bonaparte's less glorious successor: 'Le neveu ne pouvait paraître à ses yeux, comme à ceux d'un Hugo, que dérisoire caricature'.[11] In 1830, Nerval had been actively if somewhat sporadically involved, on barricades and in hospitals, as well as playing a leading role in the slightly safer 'Bataille d'Hernani' of the same year. However, in 1848, his reactions are not immediately apparent. Pierre Gascar notes, in connection with the events of this year: 'On n'avait certes aucune raison d'attendre de Gérard un net engagement politique et, encore moins, une participation physique à l'insurrection; son socialisme ésotérique—si socialisme il y a—exclut évidemment toute action violente'.[12] This confirms the picture of a Nerval whose politics were personally sympathetic, rather than radically committed. Kari Lokke asserts that

[10] The first part, 'Les Femmes du Caire', appeared in pre-revolutionary 1848, and the second, 'Les Femmes du Liban', although partly printed later in the same year, went on sale in 1850. On the effect of the 1848 Revolution on this publication, see part of the 'Notice' to *Le Voyage en Orient*, *NPl 2*, 1373–4.

[11] Jacques Bony, *NPl 2*, 1315.

[12] *Gérard de Nerval et son temps* (Paris: Gallimard, 1981), 244.

'Nerval is far from the apolitical writer and thinker most critics have assumed him to be', but this would be misleading if taken to imply a stance akin, for instance, to that of Hugo, and it is best, given the conflicting evidence there is, to proceed with some degree of caution: 'Sans doute sommes-nous mal informés des opinions de Nerval, sur lesquelles il s'est exprimé de façon contradictoire, mais il est probable que, comme la plupart des hommes de sa génération, il a vivement ressenti la désillusion qui a suivi les espoirs de 1848'.[13]

What is probably Nerval's most pointed piece of political comment started publication in *Le National* on 24 October 1850: in *Les Faux Saulniers*, he parodied the censorship and press laws which had followed the failed insurrection, while paying literal attention to their prescriptions, and drew his inspiration from immediately contemporary events. But this is not so much a radical satire on increasing authoritarianism as the expression of his humorous contempt for a legal event that hit him particularly hard as a professional writer in all genres: the passing of the Amendement Riancey. This amendment to a new law on the press had been passed on the previous 16 July, and levied a sum of one centime per copy on any newspaper that serialized a piece of fiction in its chronicle (*feuilleton*) section, a section which had traditionally been free of political comment. It was designed to stamp out the *roman-feuilleton* from the popular press: the opinion of the government, increasingly sympathetic to Louis-Napoléon, was that such popular serializations could contain a subversive amalgam of fact, fiction and comment which would incline the masses to socialist insurrection.[14] Sue's *Mystères de Paris*, a case in point, were considered to include political ideas likely to be easily impressed upon a mass readership. After the first instalment of *Les Faux Saulniers*, Nerval was promptly attacked on two fronts in *Le Corsaire* (30 October 1850): for previously collaborating with the government of Louis-Philippe and obtaining money for foreign missions, and for now becoming, in the words of the headline, 'Encore un fantaisiste qui tourne au rouge'. Although he *had* obtained missions from the previous government, Nerval publicly denied both accusations in a letter to the editor of *Le Corsaire*

[13] Kari Lokke, *Gérard de Nerval: the Poet as Social Visionary* (Lexington, Ky: French Forum, 1987), 31; Jacques Bony, *NPl 2*, 1314.

[14] See, for more details on *Les Faux Saulniers* and censorship, the 'Notice' to this text, *NPl 2*, 1314–16.

published the following day: 'Je n'ai jamais fait de politique, et ceux de mes ouvrages, pièces ou voyages où peuvent se rencontrer des paysages qui *prennent couleur*, ont toujours été écrits dans le sens libéral, comme on disait autrefois et comme on peut le dire encore aujourd'hui.'[15]

If this was to be his public stance, it is no surprise that unequivocal evidence of Nerval's attitude to the political events of these years is hard to come by. At a period when his literary ambitions were starting to bear fruit, as he thought, political upheaval may have been an unwelcome intrusion into his plans, and he may well have kept his own counsel. If these indicators of Nerval's opinion in 1850 do not point in any one direction, one cannot assume that, two years later, Nerval wished publicly to align himself with contemporary socialists (the disappointment of whose ideals had caused so much disillusionment amongst his more closely involved peers) to the extent of basing the contents of *Les Illuminés* squarely on their historical predecessors: and certainly, in the climate of 1852, this would have been a risk, more so than his mock-fearful ironizations of the Riancey proscription. 'Faut-il dire qu'il aurait été hasardeux, en 1852, de publier des études sur ces "prophètes rouges"?', notes Frank Paul Bowman: '*Les Illuminés* ne constituent pas un volume d'histoire politique, ni de polémique, mais la juxtaposition de ces textes en un volume fait néanmoins ressortir leur portée politique'.[16] This is the strongest conclusion that can be reliably drawn.

When Nerval situates his *illuminés* under the subtitle 'Precursors of socialism', his own use of the term is individualistic and based on a partly mythological image of these precursors. A prominent comment on these 'excentriques de la philosophie' in 'La Bibliothèque de mon oncle' (the preface) appears to refer to contemporary politics: 'Loin de moi la pensée d'attaquer ceux de leurs successeurs qui souffrent aujourd'hui d'avoir tenté trop follement ou trop tôt la réalisation de leurs rêves' (*NPl 2*, 885). But, given Nerval's arguable lack of any ideological stance, it is probably prudent to interpret this phrase, as Max Milner does, in a manner which puts socialism in a Nervalian context rather than the reverse: 'Le Nerval des dernières années ne semble pas avoir eu de sympathie particulière pour les socialistes... Mais ils appartiennent à la race de ceux qui ont voulu réaliser leurs

15 *NPl 2*, 1278–9 (1278); see also n. 8 and the following to this letter.

16 *Gérard de Nerval: la conquête de soi par l'écriture* (Orléans: Paradigme, 1997), 187.

rêves, et ils sont bien en cela les descendants des "excentriques" dont il est question dans *Les Illuminés*. Ceux-ci ont tous, à un moment ou à un autre, tenté d'agir sur le monde, d'imprimer à la réalité la marque de leur pensée' (*NPl 2*, 1708). The utopianism of the true *illuminé* is contrasted with Nerval's realism at this time by Jacques Bony, who again cites Milner: 'Le réalisme de Nerval est critique; il n'est pas—et peut-être le regrette-t-il—de ces écrivains qui, comme les "illuminés", "ont rêvé à un moment ou à un autre de se servir de leur plume pour transformer le réel"';[17] this is the case, at least, in the restrictedly political sphere, and true of Nerval's writing in 1852.

A Model of Illuminism

A brief sketch of the extremely complex Illuminist movement will serve to highlight why, perhaps, Nerval did not undertake to describe it in a more exhaustive manner, but it also shows to what extent *Les Illuminés* diverges from any historical model. Illuminism, in its broadest sense, was one of the sources of the imagery and thought of the Romantic movement, although what in French terms is consecutive would in Germany have been much more nearly contemporaneous, given the later date at which French Romanticism reached its height. In its most defined, narrow sense, Nerval's term would refer to the secret sect of the Illuminati, or in German *Illuminaten*, founded in 1776 in Bavaria by a former Jesuit and Professor at the University of Ingolstadt, Adam Weishaupt. It was a short-lived movement, banned by the Bavarian government in 1785, propounding republican free thought and aiming to replace Christianity with a religion of reason. Source materials for the same term also refer to a sixteenth-century Spanish mystical movement, persecuted by the Inquisition, whose members were called *Alumbrados*. As the definition is broadened, however, it becomes much more difficult to keep the discrete elements separate. A third association of the Illuminati is with the older Rosicrucians, whose founder is said by some to have been the Swiss alchemist Paracelsus (d. 1541); readers of Nerval are no strangers to this name, nor to many of those which follow. The Rosicrucians were a secret international brotherhood who claimed to possess esoteric wisdom handed down from ancient times: in their view, knowledge was only given to

[17] *L'Esthétique de Nerval* (Paris: SEDES, 1997), 112.

certain people or disciples. It was a Protestant movement. The similarities between Rosicrucianism and Freemasonry are evident, and there was a partial merger in later centuries between the two. One of the main Rosicrucian documents, *Fama Fraeternitatis* (1614), narrates the journeys of the mythical figure Christian Rosenkreuz, who acquired secret wisdom on trips to Egypt, Damascus and other points east, imparting what he knew to a limited number on his return. Other accounts of Rosicrucianism view its appearance in the sixteenth and seventeenth centuries as a revival of an order which had flourished in ancient Egypt and had been espoused by the likes of Plato, Jesus and Plotinus; for this contention there is, needless to say, no reliable evidence. It has sometimes been suggested that Descartes (b. 1596) was influenced by the Rosicrucian movement.[18] What is certain is that Illuminism (more identifiable as a current of thought than a body of specific individuals) attempted to refute the rationalistic philosophies prevalent at the time. These groupings blur, as the seventeenth century becomes the eighteenth; and individuals become easier to identify than the shifting make-up of the esoteric movements.

Paracelsus, the mystical nature-philosopher and alchemist, who derived some of his thought from the Kabbalah and Gnosticism, was a main influence upon the German mystic Jakob Boehme, who adopted the Gnostic belief that the physical world arose from a primeval fall, renewed with the historic fall of Adam. Along with the Jewish mystic Martinez Pasqualis, Boehme in turn influenced a leading exponent of Illuminism, Louis-Claude de St-Martin (1743–1803). St-Martin, described as a visionary philosopher (nicknamed *le philosophe inconnu*), having already espoused the teachings of two mystic thinkers (Boehme and Pasqualis) finally opted for a third, Swedenborg, whose influence on nineteenth-century literature is well known.

If this is a brutally concise indication of the ramified relationships between numerous different sects and personalities that are associated with Illuminism, there is no shortage of more developed treatments, all of which when dealing with Nerval come up against his minute yet eclectic erudition in this area: he would rather note similarities than analyse differences, so that the extraction of the clear entities and

[18] On Descartes and Rosicrucianism, see Stephen Gaukroger, *Descartes: An Intellectual Biography* (Oxford: Clarendon Press, 1995), 101–3, 105, 108, 113, 136.

polemics involved is no simple matter. Finally, however, it is the case that *Les Illuminés* is not generally focused on a historical description of the Illuminist movement in all its branches, though moments of intense listing and referentiality to this area become more dominant as one reads on. The volume as it stands tackles figures who are interesting in their own right and oddly eccentric (except perhaps for Jacques Cazotte), even within the deliberately *minoritaire* groupings Nerval describes, when they have any connection with this movement at all.[19]

Les Illuminés and its Sources

Not all of the source material for each *récit* is acknowledged by Nerval; nor were the materials which purport to be the sources always used directly, as references to them by the writer might lead one to suppose. However, *Les Illuminés* does seek to found itself on historically attested fact and document rather less ironically, for instance, than *Les Faux Saulniers*. Historiography is not ironized here but relativized, as might be expected from a text which presents a number of figures who seem to vindicate Nerval's interest in escaping the constrictions of conventionally conceived linear time and diachronic history. Nerval's Cazotte defies the power of time to preserve the future as a secret with his prediction of the Revolution and of his own death at the guillotine; Nerval's Quintus Aucler acts as if the Emperor Julian had succeeded in reinstating the worship of the gods of Mount Olympus, and advocates the tenets of the older form of worship as if time, for him, had indeed run a parallel course to that narrated in the history books.

The basic function of 'La Bibliothèque de mon oncle' is that of a preface. However, because the title evades the simple appellations *Préface* or *Avant-propos*, this provides an immediate clue to its potential for story-telling—as both narrative and lie—which should not be ignored. It represents the only piece of writing in the whole of *Les Illuminés* not to have appeared previously in print, and the only piece whose manuscript seems to survive, as we will see. It was written later than the pieces it precedes, although any attempt to put an exact date on its writing would be speculative. It treads a fine line, appearing

[19] See e.g. Frank Paul Bowman's comments on 'Cagliostro' and the mystical-revolutionary *Diable rouge* in general, in *Gérard de Nerval*, 140–3.

both to aim at a contemporary readership where literary portraits were the fashion—'Dans ce temps-ci, où les portraits littéraires ont quelque succès, j'ai voulu peindre certains *excentriques* de la philosophie' (*NPl 2*, 885)—and to prepare readers for what may turn out to be a very heterogeneous collection, itself eccentric, varying from purely imaginative narrative to pure plagiarism, describing a series of figures who are supposed to have caught the narrator's attention when as a child he used to roam in his uncle's attics reading books which it would not have been thought fitting to leave on more public view. It evidently functions as a lure to readers and signals what can be expected from the volume. What may perhaps be more surprising is the extent to which subsequent critics have taken the image of the uncle's library literally, going so far as to list works which it may have contained:

> Sans doute Gérard a-t-il exagéré en parlant d'une 'masse énorme' de livres. Il y avait, pensons-nous, tout au plus une dizaine de titres, ceux auxquels Nerval s'est sans cesse référé; citons, dans l'ordre chronologique: *l'Âne d'or* d'Apulée, l'*Oedipus Ægyptiacus* de Kircher (1652), *Séthos* de l'abbé Terrasson (1728), le *Dictionnaire mytho-hermétique* de Dom Pernety (1758), *le Diable amoureux* de Cazotte (1772), *le Monde primitif* de Court de Gebelin (1775–1788), *les Mémoires authentiques pour servir à l'histoire du Comte de Cagliostro* (1785), *le comte de Gabalis* de l'abbé de Villars, *les Nouvelles Recherches* de Devismes du Valgay, peut-être aussi quelque ouvrage de Chaho.[20]

This list undoubtedly points out a number of the adult Nerval's *livres de chevet*. The context in which this remark is made may, however, mislead the reader: the uncle figure is a mixture of more than one relative; the library probably existed but its contents can no longer be reliably reconstructed simply on the evidence of some mentions here and there; Richer's comment and many others like it are simply speculation, equating what were real private libraries with a fictional one which, Nerval is implying, could have housed all his source materials.[21] Nobody suggests, however, that either of the uncles who are merged into one here would have possessed the source text for 'Le Roi de Bicêtre', for instance, since it is a catalogue of sixteenth-century royal edicts drawn up by an eighteenth-century historian and lodged in the 'bibliothèque royale'.

20 Jean Richer, in *APl 2*, 937 n.3.

21 See also Max Milner's comments on this phenomenon, *NPl 2*, 886 n.1.

As well as having been read as biographically exact, 'La Bibliothèque de mon oncle' has also been read as a programmatic statement referring to the whole of Nerval's output, bypassing its specific relation to the six pieces which follow. This second attitude to 'La Bibliothèque de mon oncle' does at least demonstrate that a metaphorical or allegorical dimension has been perceived as its underlying force.[22] Ultimately, 'La Bibliothèque de mon oncle' represents Nerval's elliptical act of writing himself and his 'folies' into the margins of the volume—in other words, Nerval, in 'La Bibliothèque de mon oncle', might be said to involve himself in it as a seventh *illuminé*. 'La Bibliothèque de mon oncle', of the seven, is *the* piece which microcosmically reflects the shifting, metonymic qualities of Nerval's finer imaginative narratives. Only in a few passages do the pieces which follow qualify as portrayals of the inner dilemmas of these *illuminés*. However, this literary undertaking may have provided Nerval with a type of biographical model onto which he could subsequently inscribe his narratorial 'I'—a device which, in this work, appears only in the preface.

'Le Roi de Bicêtre', structured in a way which is simple and satisfying, displays the characteristics of self-reflexive narrative fiction rather than of any modern concept of biography. It was published in *La Presse* on 17 and 18 September 1839 as 'Biographie singulière de Raoul Spifame, seigneur Des Granges', and subsequently republished in the *Revue pittoresque* in 1845 under the title 'Le Meilleur Roi de France'. At the same period, Nerval was also interested in the mad king Charles VI ('Rêverie de Charles VI', *NPl 1*, 735–6); but traces of the play *Le Prince des sots* on the same subject disappeared within Nerval's lifetime, and the attribution of the 'novel' of the same name which is published by Jean Richer in his *Œuvres complémentaires* is now considered insecure.[23] The difference in style between 'Le Roi de Bicêtre' and 'La Bibliothèque de mon oncle' represents a leap backwards of some twelve to fourteen years (1838/9–1851/2). This is measurable, for instance, in terms of the degree of 'eccentricity' (if any) shown in narratorial tone. However, the interest this piece demonstrates in mental illness and privileged vision provides an uncanny prefiguration of Nerval's subsequent literary treatment of his

[22] Critical studies referring to a single piece, in this instance, 'La Bibliothèque de mon oncle', are discussed in the following chapter.

[23] See *NPl 1*, xvii.

own madness, linking the piece with the later Nerval more closely than the time-lapse would suggest. It is impossible to determine whether or not Nerval had a personal interest in portraying the madman Raoul Spifame as a figure worthy of esteem rather than of pity at the original date of publication, since, although Nerval was not, as far as we know, treated for mental disturbance until 1841, disturbance two years prior to this first internment cannot be ruled out.[24]

Both as a *récit* and as an unorthodox species of biography, 'Le Roi de Bicêtre' is among the most suggestively patterned, in literary as well as psychoanalytic terms, of any of Nerval's writings. This quality is due to the impression of a simple and satisfying structure, and to the device of character-doubling.[25] In fact, the doubling present has so many possibilities that it can cease to be satisfying and may seem, upon second or third reading, either to betoken a strange anxiety or to become predictable. These may be signs of immaturity in writing, or may provide evidence for the argument, still unresolved, about exactly what part Nerval played in writing the piece (which was first published over the enigmatic signature 'Aloysius'). It may have been, as it were, ghost-written by Auguste Maquet, well known as a collaborator of Dumas *père*, and a friend of Nerval, who in fact introduced them.

There are, at the very least, two points to be made against any claim Maquet might have made to *sole* authorship of the story. The actual note in which he asserts that he wrote 'Raoul Spitaine' (*sic*) has disappeared since Gustave Simon published the text of it for the first time in 1919.[26] Furthermore, it was from 1848 onwards that the collaboration between Maquet and Dumas broke up acrimoniously and that the former began to assert his legal rights to his literary property. Simon notes that Nerval was 'le grand ami, le confident, le collaborateur de Maquet' (14); but even so, Nerval must surely have been wary of publishing 'Le Roi de Bicêtre' a third time (and for the second time under his own pen-name) if there was a risk of Maquet

[24] On the biographical and literary effect of Nerval's first madness attack see e.g. Raymond Jean's comments in *Nerval par lui-même*, Collection Ecrivains de Toujours (Paris: Seuil, 1964), 34–9.

[25] Suggestively analysed by Claire Gilbert's chapter on Raoul Spifame in her *Nerval's Double: A Structural Study* (University, Mississippi: Romance Monographs Inc., 1979).

[26] *Histoire d'une collaboration: Alexandre Dumas et Auguste Maquet* (Paris: Crès, 1919).

becoming litigious.[27] I tend to think that some paragraphs of 'Le Roi de Bicêtre' are wholly due to Nerval and others to his collaborator; but there seems little doubt that 'Le Roi de Bicêtre' is broadly part of the Nervalian corpus; it is accepted as such by the exacting *Nouvelle Pléiade* editors. Nevertheless, subsequent claims here for its Nervalian textuality are made against an underlying awareness of the pitfalls of any such assumption.

As everywhere in *Les Illuminés*, the metaphorical possibilities afforded in 'Le Roi de Bicêtre' by the thematized presence of rich cloth, clothing, forms of decoration and of ornament are far-reaching. On one level, they may be taken as standing for the *text*, notable for its etymological derivation from weaving. Similarly, decoration in general produces associations with the idea of the illuminated manuscript, bearing in mind the title Nerval chose for the collection.

The final paragraph of 'Le Roi de Bicêtre', in the type of tonal *chute* often found in Nerval's work, switches abruptly from imaginative narrative into dry, historically grounded statement. Giving the title under which Spifame's decrees were actually published, *Dicaearchiae Henrici regis progymnasmata*, the narrating voice comments: 'Il en existe un exemplaire à la bibliothèque royale sous les numéros VII, 6, 412. On peut voir aussi les Mémoires de la Société des Inscriptions et Belles-lettres, tome XXIII' (*NPl 2*, 902).[28] This is comparable, for instance, with the ending of *Sylvie*: 'Pauvre Adrienne! elle est morte au couvent de Saint-S..., vers 1832' (*NPl 3*, 569), or the heavily referenced end of *Angélique* (*NPl 3*, 536).

Nerval's authoritative voice could hardly sound more precise, unless it gave page numbers. Yet it could hardly be *less* precise, a fact multiply underlined by Jean Céard's researches.[29] Spifame's forged edicts cannot be found by following Nerval's final references: 'Cette pré-

[27] The feasibility of computer-assisted analysis of language is briefly discussed in Chapter 2 (see p. 42).

[28] The first work is actually entitled *Dicaearchiae Henrici regis christianissimi progymnasmata*; the second work is, more accurately, Secousse's *Histoire de l'Académie royale des Inscriptions et Belles-Lettres, avec les mémoires de Littérature* [...], t. XXIII (Paris: Imprimerie royale, 1756).

[29] Jean Céard, 'Raoul Spifame, Roi de Bicêtre: Recherches sur un récit de Nerval', *Etudes nervaliennes et romantiques* 3 (1981), 25–50. Céard notes that Nerval probably did not consult the copy of *Dichaearchiae* brought to critical attention by Aristide Marie, but thought by Céard to have arrived too late ('plus tardivement') at the Bibliothèque Nationale for Nerval to have consulted it (49 n.9).

cision même ne doit pas faire illusion: cet exemplaire ne porte pas et ne semble pas avoir jamais porté cette cote; coté successivement F.2630, F.4588, F.1976 (cote actuelle), il a toujours appartenu à la série F; d'autre part, la B. N. n'a aucune série VII' (27). Understandably, Céard, a historian of the sixteenth century, sometimes allows a note of reproof to creep in when detailing Nerval's apparent lack of scholarship (27), his reliance on secondary sources such as the *Biographie Michaud* (29) and his apparent haste in note-transcribing (the name of the 'célèbre procureur' Noël Bruslart appears as Noël Brûlot (32)). 'Ce sont là', says Céard, referring to the use of the real names of the three 'présidents' (Liget, François de Saint-André et Antoine Ménard), 'faits d'histoire par lesquels Nerval donne une *couleur de vérité* à un récit dont l'argument principal est très librement imaginé; la belle scène du miroir, qui suit, n'est autorisée par aucune donnée historique' (34). Céard's article is not entirely error-free itself, but it certainly highlights the lack of studies of the sources of 'Le Roi de Bicêtre' up to that point.[30]

It does not, however, come back to a question touched upon on its first page: that of the authorship of the *récit*. 'En l'absence de nouveaux documents, la solution de ce problème de paternité ne peut venir que de l'examen du texte et de ses sources': but the solution is not attempted after the documents have been examined, and the writer of 'Le Roi de Bicêtre' is thenceforth referred to as Nerval 'par commodité d'exposition' (25). Since the only manuscript of *Les Illuminés* traceable to date is a draft of the prefatory 'Bibliothèque de mon oncle', Jean Céard is right to remark that decisions about the writer of 'Le Roi de Bicêtre' must be based on examination of the published text; and since Céard is clearly a historian and not a stylistic analyst, it is hardly surprising that no answer to his own question is found in his article, despite its implied claims to the contrary.

'L'Histoire de l'abbé de Bucquoy' was published for the first time only two years before its reappearance in *Les Illuminés*, and is at some remove stylistically from the smooth narration of its predecessor. This lack of evenness may in part be due to contingent factors such as the piece's extraction from *Les Faux Saulniers* and its somewhat dependent

[30] Céard's article leaves out 'les sieurs' in a citation, for instance: '[Spifame] ne fut pas fâché non plus d'avoir privé de leur office *les sieurs* Liget, François de Saint-André' (*NPl* 2, 891, italics added; Céard, 33), and does not indicate whether he is working from the version of the text published in *La Presse*, the Lecou edition or a later publication.

relationship to *Angélique*, both of which contain interpolated interventions which seem to make a virtue of its episodic qualities; but contingency does not necessarily render these qualities closed to evaluation and interpretation. Of all the *Illuminés*, 'L'Histoire de l'abbé de Bucquoy' is the most quixotic and fanciful, full of comically unrealistic markers of its status as a biographical fiction. During a life which alternates between the monastic and the military, Bucquoy is arrested for conspiring politically with some salt smugglers. His sympathies remain ambiguous, and it is never established whether the accusation is well-founded. He is confined in a series of prisons, from each of which he tries to escape, ending up in the Bastille. Sketches are given of many of his fellow prisoners, both those with whom he plots escape and the ones who betray these plots to the governors. Despite the Bastille's reputation as completely secure, he gets away. However, after fleeing the country he can never return, despite protesting his innocence through his great-aunt, the dowager countess of Bucquoy. Nerval implies, but nowhere unequivocally states, that the latter figure, an absent presence thrown into shadowy relief by her nephew's activities here, is the Angélique de Longueval of *Les Filles du Feu*. The story of her elopement with a lover of lowlier birth in *Angélique* and of the couple's subsequent travels abroad forms one strand of a similarly episodic narrative, which also takes in abridged elements of the story of Bucquoy and many of the bibliophilic anecdotes from *Les Faux Saulniers* (who are the salt smugglers mentioned above). Some of these strands also appear in *Lorely* and in *La Bohême galante*: Nerval seems to have surpassed his already considerable capacity for self-palimpsest.

Although 'L'Histoire de l'abbé de Bucquoy' is unlike 'Le Roi de Bicêtre' in its style and construction as a fictional biography, thematically the two are significantly comparable. In the former's first paragraphs the disinheritance of exiles, Protestants forced to leave lands and possessions, parallels that of younger sons like Raoul Spifame, 'un suzerain sans seigneurie' (*NPl 2*, 887). Both men's families take the decisions about what their offspring are to become, but in Nerval's interpretations the sons overturn these decisions; it seems partly to be their failure to sink gently into preordained, stable occupations that makes them the intriguing characters they are. Discussions about plagiarism and versification errors also provide links with Spifame's *fool*, Vignet ('Je suis fol', as Nerval wrote in a letter to

Houssaye);[31] and chronologically, 'L'Histoire de l'abbé de Bucquoy', situated at the turn of the seventeenth and eighteenth centuries, provides some link between the sixteenth-century *illuminé* Spifame and the remaining figures, who are from the eighteenth century. However, whereas Raoul's legal activity consists of pleading others' cases, and eventually his own, Bucquoy is hardly allowed a chance to speak by a series of judges who appear already to have decided who he is and what his crime is before he sees their faces. Whether despite or because of such ironic traits as this, the whole story seems comically unrealistic, foregrounding for example the inverse relationship between the triviality of Bucquoy's crimes (as they are presented to the reader) and the difficulty with which he is captured.

The inspiration for the story of Bucquoy looms large in *Les Faux Saulniers* and in *Angélique*, both of which, then, exist in a relationship of complicated interdependence with 'L'Histoire de l'abbé de Bucquoy'. In *Les Faux Saulniers*, an elusive volume becomes the object of a convoluted detective story similar in order and proportions to that of Poe's *Purloined Letter*. This volume's full title as given by Nerval (*NPl 2*, 4) is 'Evénement des plus rares, ou histoire du *sieur abbé comte de Bucquoy*, singulièrement son évasion du fort l'Evêque et de la Bastille, avec plusieurs ouvrages vers et prose, et particulièrement la *game* des femmes, *se vend chez Jean de la France*, rue de la Réforme, à l'Espérance, à Bonnefoy.—1719'. The version of 'L'Histoire de l'abbé de Bucquoy' published by *Le National* (as the twenty-second and final section of *Les Faux Saulniers*) contains interpolated references to the writer's detective activities, performed in order to be able to base his *feuilleton* unshakeably upon 'historical' terra firma, in mocking compliance with the recently passed Amendement Riancey. That narrative thus contains a number of comments foregrounding Nerval's *travail d'historien* which are absent from the text as it appeared in *Les Illuminés*, for instance, a footnote at the start of 'L'Enfer des vivants' (*NPl 2*, 142) deploring the lack of access to the Bastille archives,

[31] This letter is dated by *NPl* 12 Mar. 1841 (*NPl 1*, 1374–5), at the end of Nerval's first documented attack of mental disturbance, and it seems he may have been well enough here to make black humour out of his situation (Janin had just written of Nerval in the obituary past tense): 'A propos il y en a un [un Dieu] quelque part—dans un coucou—Il y en a même peut-être plusieurs—J'en ai eu peur. Mais vous allez croire mon pauvre et bon ami que je suis encore malade' (*NPl 1*, 1375). The letter had previously been dated by Richer around 20 Oct. 1854, and therefore attributed to Nerval's final fatal crisis (*APl 1*, 1123).

which according to Nerval were not available for consultation as they had not been sorted since the Revolution.[32]

The source work's title page differs, but only slightly, from the details given in *Les Faux Saulniers* by Nerval. It reads:

Evénement des plus rares | ou | l'histoire du Sr. Abbé | Comte de Buquoy [*sic*] | singuliérement | son évasion du Fort [*sic*] -l'Evêque | et de la Bastille | l'allemand à côté | revüe & augmentée, | deuxième Edition | avec | plusieurs de ses ouvrages | vers et proses | & particululiéremnt [*sic*] | La Game des Femmes | & se vend | chez Jean de la Franchise | Rüe de la Réforme à l'Espérance | à Bonnefoy | 1719

Nerval's changes amount mostly to understandable streamlining, although he has, for instance, substituted 'Jean de la France' for 'Jean de la Franchise'. The Bibliothèque Nationale catalogue, apparently following Barbier, attributes the work to Anne-Marguerite Petit, dame Du Noyer. No place of publication or publisher is given. Antoine Barbier's *Dictionnaire des ouvrages anonymes* refers to an unsigned study by Poulet-Malassis as part of an 1866 reprint, in which the book is attributed to Mme Du Noyer on the basis of its near-identity to another text, also anonymous but attributed to this author, *Lettres historiques et galantes*.[33] So the source text's identity, in the sense of its uniqueness, is anyway problematized by the existence of another work. Nerval was aware of this near-*sosie* of his authenticating source, as it is mentioned in *Les Faux Saulniers*: 'Ayant même rencontré un second récit des aventures de l'abbé de Bucquoy dans les lettres si spirituelles et si curieuses de Mme Dunoyer,—je ne me sentais pas embarrassé pour donner le portrait de l'homme et pour écrire sa biographie selon des données irréprochables.'[34] Mme Dunoyer's

[32] Daniel Sangsue (*Le Récit excentrique*) compares the eccentricities of 'L'Histoire de l'Abbé de Bucquoy', *Angélique* and *Les Faux Saulniers* with Nodier and Sterne in exemplary fashion and notes the 'woven' nature of the *récit*. Sangsue gives suggestive but extremely brief comments about *Les Illuminés* as a whole.

[33] A.-A. Barbier, *Dictionnaire des ouvrages anonymes*, 3rd edn., 4 vols. (Paris: Paul Daffis, 1872–9; photographic reprint, Paris: Maisonneuve et Larose, 1964), II (1874), cols. 333–4; Barbier gives the misprint as 'particuliclièrement'. Mme de C*** [Mme A.-M. Dunoyer], *Lettres historiques et galantes de deux dames de condition, dont l'une étoit à Paris et l'autre en province. Ouvrage curieux*, 3rd edn., 5 vols. (Cologne: Pierre Marteau, 1710–12), V (1712), 25–45. 'Province' turns out to be The Hague, at least in *Evénement des plus rares*. 'Pierre Marteau' is a fiction in itself, as it was a well-known non-existent 'cover' publisher for books which had in fact been produced in France but by appearing to be foreign evaded legal requirements, for instance those of censorship.

[34] *NPl 2*, 5–6.

narrator is a man, but he decides (after consulting an interlocutor, 'le Baron') to tell the story of Bucquoy's escape from the Bastille in the form of letters between two women.

The Abbé's story is thus set in an already paradoxical framework consisting of several layered fictions of nominal, sexual and textual identity—a possible inspiration for the ironic tone and layered, anti-chronological structure of Nerval's piece and its unreliable narrating voice. Nerval may have derived an equal amount of comic inspiration from the knowledge that his long-sought authentication, this valuable historical document which provided him with any proof he needed that he was not guilty of the literary fabrication the Amendement Riancey penalized, was itself a very deliberate *affabulation*.

'Les Confidences de Nicolas' is that most unreliable of documents, a biography based on an autobiography. The portrait by Nerval, which glosses over some of Rétif's lewder activities and transforms others into allusive musings about love of a cerebral nature, is well-known and figures regularly in critical accounts of Rétif's work.[35] There is no doubt that Nerval read in Rétif a number of philosophical and emotional concerns similar to his own, and this combines with their shared taste for prowling around Paris nightlife to provide a quite plausible argument for a common thematic and conceptual topography. However, whereas Rétif deliberately espoused direct forms of expression unprecedented in his day, and ejaculatory emotional appeals to his reader's sympathy, the third-person narration of Nerval is by turns censorious, distant and appreciative. At times, sympathy for episodes and feelings which are evidently perceived to be shared between himself and his subject add warmth and poetry to Nerval's writing; but this sympathy never compels the interventionist narrating voice to condone behaviour which could have been deemed immoral (and any sympathetic recounting of it doubly immoral). Nerval's distancing activity is very obvious (*too* obvious?) whenever the remote narrative voice periodically returns. This may enable the reader to suspend judgement, or rather may pre-empt and prevent the reader's judgement from becoming rigid. The fact that the interventions produce an ambiguous reaction does not mean, however, that their tone is ambivalent: this is far from the case.

[35] See e.g. Pierre Testud's *Rétif de la Bretonne et la création littéraire* (Geneva: Droz, 1977), and Maurice Blanchot's essay, 'Restif de la Bretonne', in *Sade et Restif de la Bretonne* (Brussels: Editions Complexe, 1986), 103–56 (first published as a preface to Rétif de la Bretonne's *Sara*, in 1949).

The form of palimpsestic activity represented by judgemental glosses and the skilful transformation of sexual references into emotional ones might be considered evidence of personal sexual *pudeur* or of fear of the censor. The immorality trials of *Les Fleurs du Mal* and *Madame Bovary* were still in the future when 'Les Confidences de Nicolas' was published in the *Revue des Deux Mondes* in August and September 1850, but they were only a few years away; however, less historicizing readings of the *récit* understandably stress its availability to psychoanalytic interpretations, given this textual strategy of erasure.

If any of the six figures represented qualifies as a visionary and a true *illuminé*, it must be Jacques Cazotte, the subject of the fourth piece. His most famous prediction, that of the forthcoming revolution of 1789 and of the execution of the King and many nobles, is only indirectly attested from an account by La Harpe, but this, as one might expect, hardly deters Nerval from spinning a tale around Cazotte's uncanny gifts and eccentric life. The 'Jacques Cazotte' to be found in *Les Illuminés* is composed of fragments that appeared in the newspapers *L'Artiste* and *La Sylphide*, and in *Almanach prophétique, pittoresque et utile pour 1847*.[36] They were simultaneously being published in Nerval's preface to a new edition of *Le Diable amoureux*, brought out by Ganivet in 1845.[37] The piece is similar to that dealing with Rétif, in that episodes are not rigorously chronological, but arranged for maximum narrative effect and significance. Thus, we read that Cazotte died at the hands of the revolutionaries before we learn of his prediction that he would do so. The subject of the 'biography' is unable or unwilling to escape the fate that the narrating voice preordains. Nerval narrates another legend attaching to Cazotte—that of his unwitting revelation of aspects of Masonic ritual, which he himself understood to have come purely from his own imagination—in the pages of *Le Diable amoureux*. When the book was published, Cazotte is said to have been approached by a shady initiate-figure, who confirmed that the rites he described were not invented, and offered to show him more: 'Je vous instruirai, je vous ferai pénétrer plus avant dans les mystères de ce monde des esprits qui nous

[36] *Almanach prophétique, pittoresque et utile pour 1847* (Paris: Aubert, [Nov. 1846]), published in two parts.

[37] 'Ganivet' was a *laitier-crémier* whose premises were used as a business address for this offshoot of the *Revue pittoresque*, and *Le Diable amoureux* is thought to have been its only publication, appearing in 30 instalments in 1845. Photographic reprint (Paris: Terrain Vague, 1960).

presse de toutes parts, et qui par l'intuition seule s'est déjà révélé à vous' (*NPl 2*, 1085).[38] If such references to cabalism and the occult reinforce the impression that Cazotte, or at least the Cazotte portrayed by Nerval, is an *illuminé*, the epithet 'précurseur du socialisme' which by implication from one of the subtitles of the whole volume ought to attach equally to Cazotte, is hardly accurate. Cazotte, unlike the majority of the guests at the occasion where he makes his prediction, is depicted anticipating the expected revolution without enthusiasm, as ushering in 'le règne fatal de l'Antéchrist' (*NPl 2*, 1105) rather than a new philosophical age. He later offers the fleeing King the sanctuary of his own residence on the way to Varennes, and his last letter to his wife and children before going to the scaffold confirms his unshaken loyalty to religion and sovereign (*NPl 2*, 1118). However, while not a socialist in a politically recognizable sense, Jacques Cazotte may have been a 'precursor' of socialism in that there is a connection to be drawn between Freemasonry, the Saint-Simonians and the socialists of 1848.

In striking contrast to the preceding materials, the sources of 'Les Confidences de Nicolas' and 'Jacques Cazotte' are relatively straightforwardly presented and documented: since the two figures involved were published writers and access to their eccentric or visionary characteristics is to be gained through their writings, Nerval sought to provide an imaginative interpretation of raw materials, as it were, which were already public. Of the three sections of 'Les Confidences de Nicolas' the first two are largely based on Rétif's autobiography, *Monsieur Nicolas, ou le cœur humain dévoilé*, published by the author in sixteen parts and seventeen volumes in 1796–7, totalling nearly 5000 pages. The third section of Nerval's *récit* analyses Rétif's character as a writer, his literary personality, and draws on a wide corpus of material, but its biographical assertions are still based on *Monsieur Nicolas*. Nerval's observations about Cazotte are taken in large part from the 1817 Bastien edition of the latter's *Œuvres* (in four volumes), with additional material from Charles Nodier's *Monsieur Cazotte* and, for the prediction, from the *Mémoires* of La Harpe.[39]

[38] This conversation is inspired by a fictional account of Cazotte's initiation, published shortly before Nerval's own *récit* by Mme d'Hautefeuille, and not factually verifiable. Max Milner points out (*NPl 2*, 1084 n.3) that *Le Diable amoureux* added nothing to what was already common knowledge. See 'La Famille Cazotte', below.

[39] *Prédiction de Cazotte, faite en 1788, et rapportée par La Harpe* (Paris: Les Marchands de nouveautés, 1817).

Nerval himself points out the unreliability of this last document, but does so in a short paragraph after a seductive *mise en scène* of the entire episode related by La Harpe, and so its rationalizing effect is negligible. In the manner of Cazotte himself and of Hoffmann, fantastical events are juxtaposed here with realistic ones, as, immediately following the prophecy and its rational rejoinder, Nerval recounts a gruesome dialogue of talking heads from Cazotte's earlier prose poem *Ollivier* (1763), which seems to prefigure the French Revolution just as effectively (*NPl 2*, 1097–9). Mme d'Hautefeuille's 'La Famille Cazotte', appearing early in 1845, preceded Nerval's Ganivet edition of *Le Diable amoureux* and his two articles in *L'Artiste* (20 April and 11 May 1845) by only a few months.[40] His use of Mme d'Hautefeuille's description of the strange initiation provides an ideal example of the possibilities of apocryphal conflation Nerval's texts seem to encourage, indicating how seductive his apparently orthodox historical narratives have proved, even to the historians themselves.

'Cagliostro' is not specifically focused around the exploits of one person: it is a condensed and subjectivized view of the foundation, history and benefits to their members of some Masonic associations, combined with a glimpse of Cagliostro's illustrious contemporary the Comte de St-Germain, and a fascinatingly embroidered anecdote describing the initiation of a group of women into a new sect headed by Cagliostro's wife. Several commentators on this collection, especially the detractors such as Barbey d'Aurevilly, remark upon the incongruity, in a study of *illuminés*, of leaving out St-Germain; and the small number of asides Nerval devotes to him, consisting of half a page in this *récit* (*NPl 2*, 1125) and sparse references to him elsewhere (for instance in 'Jacques Cazotte', and in a manuscript dating from after the publication of *Les Illuminés*)[41] can only whet the appetite. In the *Ancienne Pléiade*, Jean Richer arranged an entire dossier of items with *Les Illuminés*, under the heading 'Illuminés et Illluminisme', which, he argued, show that *Les Illuminés* was definitely intended to run to a second volume. The section included all those texts from *Le Diable*

[40] 'La Famille Cazotte', *Le Correspondant*, 1845. Published in one volume in 1846 under the pen-name of Anna-Marie. Nerval referred to Anna-Marie's article later in his series of Cazotte articles, mischievously citing a contemporaneous piece which must have been in competition with his own: 'Un auteur gracieux et plein de charme, Anna-Marie, a raconté quelques détails d'une visite faite à Pierry par Mme d'Argèle' (*NPl 2*, 1101).

[41] See below, '*Les Illuminés* and the History of Illuminism'.

rouge: Almanach cabalistique pour 1850 written by Nerval, and described as 'l'ébauche d'une galerie de portraits qui aurait constitué l'amorce d'un deuxième tome. Nerval y parle de Towiansky, Fourier, Proudhon, Pierre Leroux, Lamennais, etc. On trouvera ces textes à la suite des *Illuminés* dont ils sont le complément' (*APl 2*, 1457). Richer supports this assertion citing Nerval's letter of July 1853 to Paulin Limayrac where he attempts to justify his choice of 'Précurseurs du socialisme' as a subtitle, calling it 'un *faux titre* très réel. Je l'avais donné à l'éditeur dans la pensée d'un ouvrage plus considérable avec d'autres biographies qui ôtaient au livre le caractère que vous supposez' (*NPl 3*, 807).[42] There is no record of the intended subjects of the 'autres biographies': and yet the *Nouvelle Pléiade* editors continue to identify them as the pieces from *Le Diable rouge* (*NPl 3*, 807 n. 2). They also continue to associate the figure of the Comte de St-Germain (in the form of a very fragmentary manuscript) with *Les Illuminés* in his own right rather than as a *figurant* in 'Cagliostro' (*NPl 3*, 771 n. *a*). While much of this is credible, it is speculative, and the evidence does not suggest that Nerval was actually unhappy with the version of *Les Illuminés* which did appear.

Whatever the part St-Germain was destined to play in a non-existent volume, he appears anyway as our introduction to the lesser figure of Cagliostro, mirroring the initiatory role he is said to have played in introducing the latter to Freemasonry. Cagliostro's wife is depicted as complementing his activities, acting as hostess at a famous dinner to which prominent *philosophes* were invited and founding her Isis-worshipping sect at his suggestion, as an echo to his 'loge égyptienne' (*NPl 2*, 1125–6). Mme Cagliostro is seen as superficially a partner, but actually a protégée, of her husband. Nerval's narrating voice counterbalances and to a large extent negates the evident significance of Mme Cagliostro's sect for ideals of egalitarianism and female liberation by extensively claiming women's rapacious thirst for power and excessive curiosity. Mme Cagliostro's opening speech to her potential initiates, in which she condemns men for keeping women in a position of dependence and describes women as slaves, is referred to as 'froides plaisanteries' (*NPl 2*, 1128).

Exceptionally for *Les Illuminés*, Nerval makes no mention of any one text on which he bases his observations about the Comte de Cagliostro (whose real name, Joseph Balsamo, is also the title of one

[42] See 'Projet de publication' observations below.

of Alexandre Dumas's works on the same figure, the other being *Le Collier de la Reine*). However, Jean Richer's researches revealed that a pre-text does indeed exist: *Mémoires authentiques pour servir à l'histoire du comte de Cagliostro*, by the Marquis de Luchet.[43] This provides material which is copied verbatim into the dramatic core of this *récit*, the fourth chapter, describing the women's initiation ceremony; it is, as with the sources for Nerval's study of Rétif, much more sexually explicit than Nerval's adaptation, and includes a description of Mme Cagliostro's own initiation by sexual act, at which her husband is apparently a concealed spectator.

On its first publication in 1851, the last piece in *Les Illuminés* was entitled 'Les Païens de la République: Quintus Aucler', after having been announced as 'Le Paganisme républicain'. Containing little conventional biographical material, the piece is less a narrative than a piece of generous quotation, interspersed with explanatory linking material. 'Quintus Aucler' contains some of the most 'illuminated' writing of the whole collection, with Nerval's comparisons between Christian and 'pagan' forms of belief removing the effect of polemic from the discourse and infusing it with the syncretism with which Nerval's writing is frequently credited.

Returning to the pattern of the majority of *Les Illuminés*, this final study ('narrative' seems a misnomer) is based avowedly on Aucler's own *La Thréicie, ou la seule voie des sciences divines et humaines, du culte vrai et de la morale*,[44] which advocates a return to the polytheistic worship of the deities of classical civilizations. The difference between this last piece and the rest of the collection is in the extent to which such large sections of it are textually identical to the prose of Quintus Aucler himself.

Reading Nerval's interpretations of his sources may indeed encourage us in the conviction that literary materials can seem to respond to each other irrespective of the seductive ordering-principles of chronology and canonical literary value.[45] However, the reader's is

[43] As with the source work for 'L'Histoire de l'abbé de Bucquoy', no publisher or place of publication is mentioned, but the work is dated 1785. Luchet resembles Bucquoy in possessing a full name of somewhat magnificent proportions: Jean-Pierre Louis de la Roche du Maine, Marquis de Luchet.

[44] Paris: Moutardier, an VII (i.e. 1798 or 1799).

[45] T. S. Eliot, in 'Tradition and the Individual Talent', puts forward the view that literary works do exist in a type of atemporal dimension in which they interact with each other regardless of their diverse countries and periods of origin. He seems to

not the only perspective discernible, even if it is necessarily through this one that any others will be discerned. Authorial intention has a part to play when an anthology, of which the author appears to be the instigator, is interpreted as potentially one system. Nerval's opinion of his own work, in so far as it can be gauged from letters, has not gone unnoticed, nor has his anxiety to defend it against the unfavourable opinions of others.

Nerval's Attitude to *Les Illuminés* and the Contemporary Critical Reaction

As we have seen, *Les Illuminés* was published in late April or early May 1852, shortly before Nerval's 44th birthday, and while he was abroad, having taken out a passport for Belgium and Germany on 21 April (although the actual trip, from the evidence of letters, only took him to Belgium). Earlier in the year, when he had already notified another friend of the imminent publication of *Les Illuminés*, he had been hospitalized with what was described in medical records as 'erysipelas' after the failure of *L'Imagier de Harlem* at the newly reopened Théâtre de la Porte St-Martin. The date at which *Les Illuminés* was finally published has now been put at six months earlier than had hitherto been thought, and this prompts a reappraisal of the implications of Nerval's correspondence over the summer of 1852 and certain reviews from this time. Many references to a certain new publication which seemed, previously, to be concerned with *Lorely* (published in June by Giraud et Dagneau) can now be interpreted as allusions to *Les Illuminés* of the previous month, showing the extent of Nerval's concern to bring his new work to critical and public attention, and thus leading potentially to the discovery of further reviews by literary editors to whom Nerval wrote on the subject. One of the differences between a number of articles published separately and a volume in which they are collected is, precisely, the reviews that the latter form will attract.

A letter of 1 June 1852 shows Nerval sending a copy of an unnamed work, 'un livre qui a paru pendant mon absence', to Jules de

argue, however, that what makes them comparable is their shared character as 'great literature', thus making assumptions about a known, defined canon which imply a judgemental activity on which doubts have more recently focused. See T. S. Eliot, *The Sacred Wood: Essays on Poetry and Criticism* (London: Methuen, 1920).

Prémaray, the literary editor of *La Patrie*, who had reviewed *L'Imagier de Harlem*:

Librairie de Victor Lecou
10, rue du Bouloi
[1er juin 1852]
Monsieur,

Je ne vous ai pas encore remercié de votre charmant et si excellent article sur *L'Imagier*. J'étais alors dangereusement malade et je me suis tout à fait remis depuis en faisant un voyage dans le Nord. Voici un livre qui a paru pendant mon absence. Ne vous préoccupez d'en dire quelques mots que si cela vient dans votre cadre et sous votre plume. J'en ai un autre encore qui paraîtra dans quelques jours.

Votre bien dévoué,
Gérard de Nerval
Ce 1er juin
Suscription: A M. Jules de Prémaray à la Patrie.[46]

Six articles reviewing *Les Illuminés* are noted in *NPl 2*, but this letter leads us to a seventh, published in Prémaray's column in *La Patrie* on Tuesday 6 July 1852, and there are in fact at least nine.[47] The letter to Prémaray was overlooked precisely because the date of publication of Nerval's work of biographical fiction had long been assumed to be November (for some reason, no conclusions were drawn, for instance, from the date of the long-known article by Gautier, published in *La Presse* on 24 May 1852). Jules de Prémaray's review is not in itself remarkable, being in fact a study in saying very little, and takes up only one-fifth of the total column space of his article: that it could be discovered at this late stage, however, serves to underline that *Les Illuminés* is far from exhausted as a source of research into the historical reception of Nerval's work.

Several letters of this period may similarly be read, with the benefit of hindsight, as pertaining to *Les Illuminés* rather than to their previously assumed referent, *Lorely*. Commenting on the letter already cited, Jules Marsan notes that 'la lettre de Gérard a été écrite entre l'apparition de *Lorely* et celle des *Illuminés*', whereas the reverse is the

46 Letter cited in the form given in *Gérard de Nerval: Correspondance (1830–1855)*, ed. Jules Marsan (Paris: Mercure de France, 1911), letter LXXIII, 178–9. The version given in *NPl 2*, 1306 reproduces the *en-tête* and *suscription* only in notes.

47 Those by Gautier, Prémaray, the Goncourts, Limayrac, Asselineau, Bell, Lewes, Barbey and Pontmartin; see Appendices, which include the full text of Prémaray's review.

case.[48] In his letter to Prémaray, Nerval's tone is diffident—showing a cool disinterest better in keeping with conventional professional interactions than, for instance, the tone of 'La Bibliothèque de mon oncle', already remarked upon for its personal urgency, as Nerval in the persona of narrator desires his book to hold the potential promise of everything his unknown reader might wish to find within its pages. Two days after the letter to Prémaray, Nerval's epistolary style is equally reserved when writing to Janin, who had contributed reviews to *Les Débats*: 'Vous devez avoir reçu celui de Lecou' (*NPl 2*, 1307). Janin had already been sent a review copy: it bore a dedication reading 'A Jules Janin (que j'ai connu chez Nodier). Hommage reconnaissant, Gérard de Nerval'.[49] That Nerval felt he could write a dedication—to Janin—in his latest volume suggests that he was satisfied with it, and was happy openly to associate himself with it; and this must in turn suggest that Nerval thought it did not provide further ammunition for those, such as Janin, whose public comments on his mental condition had caused his reputation so much damage in the past. There is no known review by Janin in response to this gesture.

On or just after 16 June, Nerval sent another copy of *Les Illuminés* to Emile de Girardin, but he only refers to it in the postscript of a letter of this date, adding: 'Je n'ai pas besoin de vous avertir qu'il y a quelque ironie dans la préface sur ce sujet semi-politique du socialisme—à moins que vous ne lisiez pas l'ouvrage' (*NPl 2*, 1307–8). Providing as it does one of Nerval's few 'glosses' of the subtitle 'Précurseurs du socialisme', this comment has been cited many times. It seems to me to indicate above all else that we cannot accurately fathom the several layers of irony present in Nerval's comment here; it would be unwise to orientate a reading of the subtitle or of 'La Bibliothèque de mon oncle' entirely around such a comment. Nerval knew he was writing to a man who had recently published an attack upon socialism; he nevertheless wished Girardin to read his book, and

[48] *Gérard de Nerval: Correspondance*, 317 n.144. It has already been noted that *Lorely* was published in June 1852 by Giraud et Dagneau. Since Nerval wrote to Prémaray, enclosing a review copy, from Victor Lecou's business address, it seems reasonable to suppose that the volume in question was *Les Illuminés*, not *Lorely*, and that Nerval had called at Lecou's expressly to obtain review copies, as soon as he returned from abroad. The letter to Prémaray in fact provides one of the first pieces of evidence that Nerval had returned.

[49] The discovery of this dedication is due to Jean Richer, who found a copy of *Les Illuminés* thus marked in an auction catalogue (*NPl 2*, 1307, n. 3).

his ambiguous utterances are equal to the task of confusing the issue sufficiently.[50] One of the postscript's most evident ironies is, of course, the use of 'je n'ai pas besoin de vous avertir', performing the act whose necessity it denies.

A letter encouraging and obtaining a review of a new book, a dedication in another copy, and a postscript accompanying a third, plus the reviews: shards of evidence such as these hold up, as it were, a fractured mirror to the fragmented forms coexisting within *Les Illuminés* and to the dissections it has subsequently undergone as a reaction to its forms. The cumulative effect of Nerval's notes circulating the news of his latest publication nevertheless supports the view that his ambition for and seriousness towards his own writing was on the increase at around this time. From the age of 19, he had been accustomed to seeing his name, in its various guises, in print, but, as we have seen, the first volume to consist fully of his own narrative prose (*tirés à part* of individual, smaller items excepted) was his *Scènes de la vie orientale* (1848). Jean Richer comments, in a Notice to *Les Filles du Feu*, on what he sees as a lack of inspiration on Nerval's part:

> Depuis deux ans, Gérard a publié coup sur coup cinq volumes qui comptent parmi les meilleurs de son œuvre: le *Voyage en Orient*, *Les Illuminés*, *Lorely*, les *Contes et Facéties*, enfin les *Petits Châteaux de Bohême* [...] Mais il n'est aucun de ces volumes qui ne soit fait pour une bonne part de pages plus ou moins anciennes, reprises aux périodiques où elles étaient dispersées. On sent qu'à tout prix, inquiet sur ses facultés d'invention, Nerval veut prouver au public, à ses amis, et surtout à lui-même, qu'il est autre chose qu'un feuilletoniste parisien et un auteur de bluettes agréables. Quitte à se répéter [...] il faut qu'il produise au grand jour. (*APl 1*, 1176)

It may be possible to detect a lack of selectiveness in the choice of material for *Les Filles du Feu* (1854, a volume which included *Les Chimères*), indicating excessive haste as Nerval was panicked by increasingly serious bouts of mental disturbance, although it is equally plausibly read as a deliberate confounding of the bounds of the prose *récit*. And although *Les Illuminés* bears the marks of some expediency, this is not the only or overriding impression that can be gained.

[50] Emile de Girardin, *La Politique universelle: décrets de l'avenir* (Brussels: C. Muquart, 1852): see *NPl 2*, 1308 n.1. At around the same period, Girardin published *L'Empereur Napoléon III et l'Europe*, which ran to nine printings in a single year.

One of the contemporary critical assessments in which *Les Illuminés* found a place, that of Paulin Limayrac, takes a broader view of Nerval's work, paralleling his increasingly voluminous appearances in print. Both this review and that by Barbey d'Aurevilly take issue with Nerval in detail, and they prove the most extensively argued, while another, by Pontmartin, is merely dismissive. Further proof that Nerval had started to become aware of the corpus his work now represented is found in a letter of around 13 July 1853 to Gervais Charpentier, in which Nerval is in the process of sending as much of his work to Limayrac as possible in anticipation of a forthcoming piece: 'Il veut me faire un article, pour moi seul, samedi en huit. Je lui envoie toutes mes œuvres. Envoyez donc la principale à *La Presse*, sous son nom.' Two weeks later, on 31 July, Nerval writes a well-known response to Limayrac's accusations of scepticism, a more highly charged term then than now, and gives yet another ambiguous clue to his intentions in choosing his subtitle:

> Mon cher Limayrac,
>
> Je me jette à vos genoux de critique, sauvez-moi de l'envie, vous qui répandez la lumière et qui lancez la foudre. Comment vous remercier? En regrettant d'abord de m'être exposé à votre seule critique, et cela par négligence. Le titre *Précurseurs du socialisme* est un *faux titre* très réel. Je l'avais donné à l'éditeur dans la pensée d'un ouvrage plus considérable avec d'autres biographies qui ôtaient au livre le caractère que vous supposez; ... J'aurai aussi peut-être à démontrer plus tard que l'affirmation est le résultat du *doute*, et que je ne suis pas si sceptique qu'il le paraît.[51]

This letter bears the same date as the issue of *La Presse* in which Limayrac's disinterested article appeared. The article includes in its broad sweep not only *Les Illuminés* but *Le Voyage en Orient*, *Petits Châteaux de Bohême* and *Lorely*.

Another possible article, by Charles Monselet, is mentioned by Nerval himself in a letter to Louis de Cormenin dated to the end of 1852 (*NPl 3*, 796), but this review has not so far come to light. Nerval writes: 'Mon cher Cormenin, Voici Monselet que vous connaissez, qui a fait un article sur *Les Illuminés*, qui n'est pas tout en ma faveur, à ce qu'il dit, mais j'aime mieux cela, et au contraire s'il se trompait, il faudrait en rajouter.' Monselet did, however, write a largely complimentary assessment of 'Les Confidences de Nicolas' in his own

[51] Note to Charpentier dated around 13 July 1853 (*NPl 3*, 804); letter to Limayrac, already mentioned, 31 July 1853 (*NPl 3*, 807).

study on Rétif de la Bretonne, noting that Nerval's only mistake is to emphasize the man and his perceived moral turpitude over the writer and thus to prejudice the validity of his own study.[52]

Finally, there is a gratifyingly long and serious discussion of the volume by Asselineau from *L'Athenæum français*, showing interest in questions that are still critically relevant. It begins and concludes on generic considerations, at first potentially complimentary ('Ce genre de collection est aujourd'hui à la mode, encore est-on bien heureux quand ces éléments ainsi réunis ont entre eux autant d'analogie que ceux du présent volume'), then unconvinced ('L'auteur serait-il d'avis que tous les fous sont des illuminés?'), takes a diversion into a diatribe against *realists*, links illuminists and revolutionary activity unequivocally and finally returns to the difficulty of reading these portraits with any expectations of generic fixity: 'Néanmoins la difficulté de les relier entre eux, par l'absence d'une méthode primordiale, ne laisse pas de créer des embarras sérieux pour l'esprit, dès qu'on essaye de remonter de l'effet à la cause. Pourquoi M. Gérard de Nerval ne se dévouerait-il pas jusqu'à donner une histoire, un tableau des idées mystiques modernes?'[53] These expectations have been vexing well-intentioned readers ever since.

Evidently, critical opinion of the time was much taken up with the ideas of sincerity, authenticity and truth in art, and, as far as the majority of his reviewers were concerned, Nerval had appeared to nail his colours to the mast of the school of Realism. It is not clear that Nerval would have shared this opinion. The letters cited above are ambiguous, as is 'La Bibliothèque de mon oncle', combining an unashamed bid for contemporary popularity—'Dans ce temps-ci, où les portraits littéraires ont quelque succès' (*NPl 2*, 885)—with uses of vocabulary designed to attract the attention of avid realists. Nerval none the less indicates that some may find his book quirky, thus preparing those who wish to proceed for the esoteric nature of what follows. Limayrac and Barbey, reproaching Nerval's work with scepticism, are castigating him for attitudes which elsewhere call up praise. As a philosophical term, from which its looser general usage derives, scepticism involves the refusal of any absolute certitude (Littré

[52] The essay is reprinted in *Oubliés et Dédaignés: Linguet, Fréron, Rétif de la Bretonne, Mercier, Cubières* (Paris: Bachelin-Deflorenne, 1885); Michel Brix gives references to its first publication in his 'Nerval, *Les Illuminés* et le scepticisme', *Romanische Forschungen* 106 (1994), 1–4, 243–53, and I am also indebted to him for drawing my attention to Asselineau's review.

[53] *L'Athenæum français* (28 Aug. 1852), 132–3.

adjoins the *dicton* 'Doutez de tout'). A consequence of this is 'une mise en doute des dogmes religieux' (*Petit Robert*). Barbey, the more polemic critic of the pair, asks: 'M. Gérard est-il un sceptique? Sait-il ou ne sait-il pas? Croit-il ou ne croit-il pas? [...] S'il est sceptique comme le siècle dont il est le fils, il n'a pas le style qui doit embaumer cette misérable larve d'un esprit qui n'ose pas vivre'. These comments are occasioned by the figures in the volume who practise or advocate unorthodox religions, those who doubt, in the terms of the *Robert* definition. Paulin Limayrac's piece is written more in sorrow than in anger: he thinks the motive for the choice of figures both coherent and sinister: 'Si c'étaient des biographies prises au hasard, il faudrait tout simplement, et sans plus de réflexions, se donner le plaisir de la lecture. Mais non, ce ne sont pas des biographies prises au hasard; une pensée philosophique a présidé à ce choix.' Limayrac does not have only adverse criticism, and shows a certain discriminating *justesse* in his choice of terminology to classify the pieces: 'Les *Confidences de Nicolas* sont arrachées toutes vivantes de l'histoire de la fin du XVIIIe siècle. La vie de Cagliostro, qui est une comédie, et la vie de Cazotte, qui est une élégie, sont l'une et l'autre supérieurement racontées [...] On voit qu'il y a de la matière de qualité dans ce livre, sans compter que presque d'un bout à l'autre il pétille d'érudition, si l'on me passe le mot.'

Armand de Pontmartin's 'Les Historiens de l'illuminisme' makes a comparison between three books on similar subjects, of which Nerval's comes off the worst. The other two are Caro's *Du mysticisme au XVIIIe siècle: Essai sur la vie et la doctrine de St-Martin* and Henri Delaage's *Le Monde prophétique*. The reader will match each author with Pontmartin's opening cryptic clues, so Nerval could be any one of the following: 'Un penseur judicieux et profond, un charmant songeur, un curieux et spirituel sceptique'.[54] After the references to the 'spirituel' and 'curieux' qualities of Nerval's work, epithets which it seems to attract regularly, Pontmartin imagines leading Delaage (whom he treats as young and inexperienced, but worthy of instruction) safely through its moral snares:

[54] *Causeries littéraires* (Paris: Michel Lévy frères, 1854), 185–96 (185). Reproduced in its entirety by Henri Bachelin in the Bernouard edition of *Les Illuminés* (1929), 411–19. Delaage collaborated with Nerval to write articles in record time for *Le Diable rouge: Almanach cabalistique* of 1849. See *NPl 1*, 1926 and Ch. 2 here.

> Que M. Delaage relise avec nous le livre, si spirituel et si curieux, où M. Gérard de Nerval nous raconte l'histoire des *Illuminés, précurseurs du socialisme*, et qu'il nous dise s'il n'y a pas eu, dans les sciences occultes, tout un côté dangereux, chimérique, véreux, taré, mêlé d'impudence, d'escroquerie et de mensonge, le côté des libertins comme Restif, des fous comme Raoul Spifame, des fripons comme Cagliostro, renfermant en germe le saint-simonisme, le fouriérisme, le communisme, c'est-à-dire, encore et toujours, la révolte, le dogme et l'apothéose de la matière. (196)

Pontmartin's political and moral stance could not be clearer, especially coming in the wake of his eulogy of Caro's work: 'Si vous m'en croyez, nous ne mépriserons pas le mysticisme, surtout quand il a M. Caro pour historien et pour interprète' (196). What distinguishes his argument is that, evidently, he does not disagree with Nerval's implied classification of all six figures as *illuminés*, although his sub-classes of 'fous', 'fripons', and 'libertins' indicate that he may be more concerned to be dismissive than discerning. But despite Pontmartin's bias, his emphasis on the danger inherent in Nerval's choice of subject echoes the arguments of Barbey and of Limayrac.

If the observations in these reviews can be taken as an accurate reflection of the literary preoccupations of the time, especially the debate about the value of realism and how far it should be taken, then Barbey, Pontmartin and Limayrac represent the sceptics; or rather, they are sceptical about scepticism, which they believe realism is implicated in spreading. Gérald Schaeffer, in *Une Double Lecture de Gérard de Nerval*, emphasizes the realist leanings of *Les Illuminés*, although he differentiates Nerval's interpretation of it from that of the most committed zealots of the new stylistic ideology, amongst them the Goncourts, whose review is discussed below. Realism in the arts and socialism in political sympathies were to some extent taken as part of the same phenomenon, both by opponents and supporters, although ironically the stipulations of the Amendement Riancey, which was part of the anti-socialist political backlash after 1848, may have contributed to the development of realism, with its emphasis on a constructed, 'believable', contemporary subject matter and apparently simple style. Since the subtitle of *Les Illuminés* refers to socialism, it is even more tempting to associate this possible political indicator with a cognate literary indicator and to read more realism into the lines of this work than is strictly justified. Nerval's contemporaries may be better judges of his sympathies with the dictates of literary style and legal obligation: in statistical terms, three of the reviews criticize the work in question for its socialist or realist sympathies, one praises it for the same perceived tendencies, and four praise it because they are sympathetic to Nerval. Hardly a conclusive verdict.

Critical preferences for particular figures amongst the six point to similar conclusions about the prevailing literary climate and Nerval's place in it. When reviewers do select particular figures for comment and praise, their choice often lights on Rétif de la Bretonne. This is true of the Goncourts, and of Gautier, in whose article this story alone is mentioned especially: 'Les *Confessions* [sic] *de Nicolas*, le morceau le plus dévéloppé du volume, a tout l'intérêt du roman le plus vif, le plus attachant: les multiples amours de Restif de la Bretonne y sont réunies dans un cadre ingénieux et marchent de pair avec la vie littéraire de ce Balzac du ruisseau, qui semble avoir deviné les *Mystères de Paris* avant Eugène Sue et le *Phalanstère* avant Fourier.' Georges Bell, in the *Mercure de France*, is again of this opinion. In a brief description of each sketch, he refers to Rétif as a man of some note, 'dont le nom rappelle toute une époque passée dans ses livres, palpitants de réalisme, avec ses vices, ses vertus, ses crimes, ses lâchetés, ses hypocrysies [*sic*]'. The development of this opinion makes it clear that Bell's preference is dictated by the amount of gritty 'realistic' social observation he discerns in Rétif: 'Dans cette série de figures, la plus importante, la plus intéressante, à coup sûr, est celle de Nicolas Restif de la Bretonne. Avec un art infini, Gérard de Nerval a su raccorder la vie si accidentée de cet homme qui ne recula devant rien, vice, crime, dégradation, pour arriver à connaître ses semblables.' Passing from the personality of Rétif to the skill of his biographer, Bell comments: 'Son entrée en matière ressemble à un premier chapitre de roman; on dirait une mise en scène arrangée à plaisir. Et cependant tout est vrai, jusqu'au moindre détail.' G. H. Lewes, in *The Westminster and Foreign Review*, also prefers the same piece, commenting after he has given the briefest of descriptions of 'Le Roi de Bicêtre' and 'L'Histoire de l'Abbé de Bacquoy [*sic*]': 'But amusing as these are, they are nothing compared with the story of "Restif de la Bretonne", the once popular romancist, of whom Gérard de Nerval has written a biography more interesting than a novel'.[55] This article is given as anonymous by the editors of *NPl 2*: however, it is relatively simple to

[55] [G. H. Lewes], 'Contemporary Literature of France', *The Westminster and Foreign Review* (1 Oct. 1852), 614–30 (629).

provide it with an attribution by consulting the *Wellesley Index to Victorian Periodicals*.[56] A *romancist* is a romantic novelist: the novel is a form hard to surpass in interest, but in taking as his subject a novelist, Nerval has managed to combine his own and Rétif's skill in this field with a different, and perhaps in itself novel, transformation into biography.

Whenever this 120-page narrative is compared with a novel, the comparisons are intended to be complimentary. Limayrac describes *Les Illuminés* as 'un recueil de biographies tournées en roman'. In addition to his comment already mentioned referring to Rétif, G. H. Lewes also opens his paragraph of commentary with the words: 'Another book, also a reprint, *Les Illuminés*, by Gérard de Nerval, is worth half a dozen novels.' Pointing to a desire on the part of the critics to see the piece on Rétif as subsumed into the lengthier novel genre to which it does not, in its given state, conform, these observations reflect the links between the rising star of realism and the novel, already in its ascendant. Lewes's is virtually the only assessment not to predicate qualities of authenticity and truth-to-life (especially its less pleasant aspects, as seen in Bell's comment on Rétif) onto this work. The Goncourts note that there are episodes 'd'une grâce, d'une jeunesse, d'un sentiment, d'une *vérité*, d'un poignant' in the long and chequered career of Rétif.[57] Jules de Prémaray notes: 'Eminemment poète, M. Gérard de Nerval voit les choses par leur vrai côté', and Bell chimes in with his 'tout est vrai' cited above.

A number of further comments refer metaphorically to sibling arts such as painting: 'On dira que ce n'est que de la peinture de genre: c'est de l'excellente et fine peinture' (Limayrac on *Le Voyage en Orient* in his combined review); 'On dirait une mise en scène arrangée à plaisir' (Bell). What may be more unexpected are two other refer-

[56] See *Wellesley Index to Victorian Periodicals 1824–1900*, ed. Walter E. Houghton, 5 vols. (Toronto and Buffalo: University of Toronto Press, 1979). Arranged in the form of one chapter per periodical, it lists the 'Westminster' under various names (*Westminster Review*, *Westminster and Foreign Review*, *Westminster and Foreign Quarterly Review*). Lewes's article is to be found in vol. 3, p. 618, no. 1327.

[57] Italics added. Their precious style, both here and in the editor's 'manifesto' inaugurating *L'Eclair* in January of the same year, belies their declared intent to do away with rhetorical devices: 'La vérité toujours, la vérité en tout et pour tout. Ce langage paraîtra nouveau: en effet, nous nous vantons de posséder une qualité nouvelle: la conscience [...] Guerre aux paradoxes! gloire à la verité' (*L'Eclair*, 10 Jan. 1852, 1).

ences, one to a kind of science and one to a new form of technology. A metaphor of Gautier's recalls the seventeenth- and eighteenth-century study of physiognomy, combining it with a more contemporary search for reality in literature—which translates as a desire to bring forth the unknown and the incongruous: 'Il y a là tout un côté inconnu du dix-huitième siècle découvert pour la première fois, une foule de détails qu'on ne trouve nulle part, des physionomies esquissées avec une réalité singulière'. Gautier's enthusiasm for the realistic portrait hints at a cultural reference to one of the great technological innovations of the nineteenth century, which the Goncourts make explicit: 'Cette étude, qui prend Restif presque à sa naissance et le conduit à sa mort, est un des plus charmants *daguerréotypes* littéraires que nous ayons' (italics added); enthusiasm for this medium is much more muted in the case of Nerval himself, however, in his avowed attempt at a Realist text: 'Le daguerréotype, instrument de patience qui s'adresse aux esprits fatigués, et qui, détruisant les illusions, oppose à chaque figure le miroir de la vérité'.[58]

The examination of the reviews available is a crucial step towards situating *Les Illuminés* in its contemporary framework; some of their comments may merely indicate how Nerval's work could be susceptible to an unduly politicized (or, at least, polarized) reading, regardless of its apparently atemporal subject matter. It is notable that the most cogently argued assessments are those of the detractors; Philippe Lejeune observes this same phenomenon, in connection with the critical reception of *Victor Hugo raconté*: 'Les éreintements sont plus instructifs que les éloges sur la situation du livre dans les "horizons d'attente" de l'époque'.[59] A politically engaged intention seems, however, ultimately unprovable without further evidence, and this is certainly the case when one compares *Les Illuminés* with the much more perceptible slant of *Les Faux Saulniers*.

Perhaps the most suggestive comments in all these reviews are, however, those which deal with the fact-fiction axis, especially with reference to the perception of the six *récits* as biographies. It should be clear from the relations between given historical data, Nerval's source materials and the literary productions published collectively as *Les Illuminés* that the only means by which 'history' and 'source' can be accounted for in these productions is via the intertextual matrix,

[58] *Les Nuits d'octobre*, *NPl 3*, 322; also in a letter to Georges Bell.

[59] *Je est un autre: l'autobiographie de la littérature aux médias* (Paris: Seuil, 1980), 66.

within which mythical, literary and imaginative resources have an equal, if not greater, force. The insidious inclusion of Nerval's work within the spectrum of the novel, performed already by his contemporaries, merely highlights the necessity for an investigation of it as narrative fiction: as a number of fictions, but also as *one* fiction.

CHAPTER 2

The Text and its Readers

What have the twentieth-century readers of Nerval, the successors of Barbey and the Goncourts, made of *Les Illuminés*? In his critical bibliography of 1968, James Villas concludes with a section entitled, in a phrase reminiscent of Nerval's own, 'Projets à faire': he proposes a number of lines of enquiry some of which have not been fully pursued even today. He states that 'No significant study has yet been devoted to *Les Illuminés*, an extremely complex work which leads the reader into Nerval's strange esoteric world and that illustrates further the poet's narrative technique'.[1] None of the major studies of Nerval's esotericism fulfils Villas's criterion of being devoted to *Les Illuminés* as a whole, although Jean Richer's *Nerval: Expérience et Création* contains numerous references to most of the figures; but, under Richer's influence, what interest there was often relied heavily on the esoteric themes in this work, perhaps because of the book's formal heterogeneity, rather than focusing on poetics or the narrative technique mentioned by Villas. However, more recently, this tendency has begun to be reversed.

What is available to us, then, if we are intent on a re-evaluation of *Les Illuminés* now, anticipating a new century and the bicentenary of Nerval's birth? Much of the critical material available is located in editorial introductions and notes, rather than in separate publications; not many insights can now be gleaned from manuscript material; a single book and a number of articles deal with *Les Illuminés* as a whole; and a further group single out one or two of the pieces for consideration. Some rather more general studies also refer to *Les Illuminés* in passing, yet they almost never support a lengthy interpretation, or even encourage a cover-to-cover reading, while other works have been painstakingly remodelled according to the available data on

[1] James Villas, *Gérard de Nerval: A Critical Bibliography 1900–1967* (Columbia, Missouri: University of Missouri Press, 1968), 30.

Nerval's intentions and drafts (*Aurélia* and *Pandora*, for instance) or reconstructed in their fullest forms (*Les Faux Saulniers*), apparently in order that just such a reading can be made possible.

Manuscripts

The only surviving manuscript relating to *Les Illuminés* consists of a draft of 'La Bibliothèque de mon oncle', the sole piece of the book not to have been published before the 1852 volume.[2] It is consistent with contemporary journal editors' practice of not conserving manuscripts after their publication in *feuilleton* form that the handwritten copies of each individual piece should have been thrown away, destroyed or otherwise lost after their first publication, so that it would be an unlikely, if welcome, bonus should they come to light in the future. The *Nouvelle Pléiade* gives a full description of a manuscript draft of 'La Bibliothèque de mon oncle' (*NPl 2*, 1711–12), which renders further detail unnecessary here, except in so far as it offers a superb example of Nerval's graceful streamlining in revisions.[3]

If drafts of 'Le Roi de Bicêtre' were found, they might solve at once the continuing mystery surrounding Auguste Maquet's involvement with its creation. Maquet is more famous as a collaborator of Dumas's, and eventually took Dumas to task in order to reclaim some of his authorial and financial rights. In the absence of any such helpful manuscript, perhaps the only method of reaching a viable conclusion on the question of authorship would consist of a computer-aided frequency-comparison of syntactic and lexical patterning between this story and the writings of Nerval and Maquet independently. However, in practice, it proves hard to achieve a reliable result from such a procedure: material for comparison would have to be drawn from a chronologically, generically and above all thematically comparable corpus of Nerval's writing, which does not truly exist in the amount required; and to compound this difficulty, there is the added problem of the scarcity of material written only by Maquet.

Finally, the lack of manuscripts means that the possibilities for genetic criticism, for instance, are extremely limited in relation to *Les Illuminés*, unless in the broader sense that the singly published versions

[2] The MS forms part of the Collection Spoelberch de Lovenjoul, now located in the Institut français in Paris, though previously in Chantilly.

[3] See the short descriptions of each piece above, and 'Une Préface élusive' below.

of the pieces show a degree of shift that has often intervened between them and the 1852 text.[4]

Oldest and Newest Editions of *Les Illuminés*

As we have seen, the first edition of 1852 published by Victor Lecou bears the dubious distinction of having provided *Les Illuminés* with alternative subtitles, one figuring on the title page and the other on the cover. The former, 'Récits et portraits', is rather overshadowed by its more controversial counterpart, 'Précurseurs du socialisme'. But 'Récits et portraits' is, to me, just as interesting and ambiguous: its simplicity, implying that *Les Illuminés* follows in a well-trodden rut as far as generic distinction goes, is belied, and our assumptions are confounded by the diversity of the narratives.

This is not a noticeably well-produced or luxurious edition, although many of the glaring errors of the serial publications are eradicated. In some libraries, consultation of the actual volume, rather than microfilm, is not encouraged. However, consultation of the physical object is in many respects preferable: it alerts us, for instance, to the fact that binding the flimsy paper cover would neatly obliterate the politically contentious subtitle, leaving 'Récits et portraits' in a position of prominence.

The most recent edition of *Les Illuminés* to publish new textual scholarship is that of the *Nouvelle Pléiade*, on which I have drawn substantially. The general editors, Jean Guillaume and Claude Pichois, base their versions on the most complete versions of texts published during Nerval's lifetime, and thus here on Lecou. The *Nouvelle Pléiade* is for the most part extremely textually accurate, as one might expect. This is complemented by a noticeable effort to reproduce original punctuation (such as the characteristic long dash): some changes are made for the sake of general Pléiade practice concerning the modernization of punctuation and spelling (in the first few pages of 'Le Roi de Bicêtre', 'différens', 'vêtemens' and the like, various commas and capitals, are changed compared with *La Presse* and Lecou), but this is still a vastly preferable research tool to the previous alternatives.

[4] For discussion of manuscript study in the case of Nerval, see *Nouvelle Pléiade* critical material in general, and a broad introduction to the issues by Peter J. Edwards, 'Problèmes d'études de manuscrits: le cas de Nerval', in *Sur la génétique textuelle*, ed. D. G. Bevan and P. M. Wetherill (Amsterdam: Rodopi, 1990), 55–63.

Max Milner's extended essay on *Les Illuminés* here is both lucid and yet in sympathy with the intuitive relationships Nerval sets up between the six quite different figures ('Notice', *NPl 2*, 1696–1709). One of the main threads running through the essay is a discussion of the tension between analysis (or fragmentation) and synthesis, between encodings of anatomy and of identity in this work, within the terms of its biographical project. Biographical narrative in the mid-nineteenth century is very much the sibling of the abundant Dictionaries of contemporary figures, and both are indicative of nineteenth-century France's growing quasi-scientific preoccupation with its own anatomization in portraits, encyclopaedias and 'physiologies'.[5] Since Milner discerns in *Les Illuminés* a 'véritable unité stylistique' (1708), his own comments maintain a careful distance from the compartmentalization of the *anatomie*, an enumeration-by-figure which so often seems unavoidable.[6] Although in practice he emphasizes the narratives of Rétif's and Cazotte's lives more heavily than the rest (a tendency shared with Gérald Schaeffer's reading and the positions adopted by Binder and Jaton below), his study does concentrate on conceptual areas which cross and re-cross the whole text 'de façon suffisamment significative pour concourir à sa tonalité propre et justifier l'impression paradoxale d'unité' (1701).[7] The areas of interconnection he perceives also coincide with much of Nerval's other work, and include madness, the feared death of faith, mediations between different epochs in history, the cathartic aspects of writing, the challenge of realism, wariness of direct self-revelation, literary narcissism and the double. Milner's final opinion is that, although in the case of Rétif the *travail de transformation* is remarkable, this is in the name of *pudeur*, and that on the whole Nerval carries out no exorbitant modifications of the texts he adapts. Yet we find to our

[5] See e.g. the following consecutive entries: 'La biographie contemporaine', 'Publications encyclopédiques et recueils collectifs', 'Des études de mœurs à la caricature, au portrait-charge' and 'Un genre particulier: les "Physiologies"', in Madeleine Ambrière (ed.), *Précis de littérature française du XIXe siècle* (Paris: PUF, 1990), 152–60.

[6] To some extent, the analytical process entails such fragmentation, and procedures in the present study are part of a similar fragmenting process. Gérald Schaeffer's *Double Lecture* is superficially structured entirely along the lines of an 'Anatomy'.

[7] On the use of the spelling 'Rétif' instead of 'Restif', I follow the argument advanced by Pierre Testud at the beginning of *Rétif de la Bretonne et la création littéraire.*

surprise that 'il en résulte non seulement une unité de pensée, mais, mis à part quelques passages plus faibles, une véritable unité stylistique [...] dont seule une étude linguistique approfondie pourrait rendre compte. Peut-être révélerait-elle dans cette impression une part d'illusion' (1708–9). Far from revealing itself as illusory, Milner's impression of stylistic interconnection seems to be confirmed when closer attention is paid to the poetics and narrative techniques which can be discerned in *Les Illuminés*. Milner's essay is inspiring and refreshing in its affirmation that much remains to be said and thought about *Les Illuminés*, and also about 'la plasticité et [...] l'extraordinaire pouvoir d'accueil' which Nerval allied to his 'vaste culture' (1709).

Milner's study highlights the absence, then, of an 'étude linguistique approfondie', but seems also to leave to one side the notion of literary form or genre, contenting itself with the term 'études' to describe the parts of the book, and thus perhaps over-emphasizing its claims to historical scholarship. It also gives references to the Maquet controversy over 'Le Roi de Bicêtre' in several different places[8] without, apparently, addressing the real possibility that at least some of the story did originate from Maquet, and this highlights a grey area in the general editorial policy of the *Nouvelle Pléiade*. Maquet's name is conspicuous by its absence from the 'declaration of policy' by Guillaume and Pichois, enunciated in the preface to the first volume, where they reject much of what is written in collaboration, not only the plays but also for instance the *chroniques* signed 'G.-G.' or 'G.' in selected publications because they were at least partly written with Gautier and others:

> Sont recueillis dans les trois volumes de cette nouvelle édition [...] tous les textes que Nerval a explicitement ou implicitement reconnus comme siens. Explicitement, par une de ses signatures avérées. Implicitement, par un témoignage indubitable, qu'il soit de lui ou d'un contemporain. Cet adverbe ne saurait désigner un texte anonyme ou signé d'un pseudonyme dans lequel se trouverait une idée, une image, un thème contenu dans un texte qui est de Nerval. (*NPl 1*, xiv)

The plays are rejected because of their having been written with others. And yet, Nerval seems very much to have 'recognized' some of them, especially *Léo Burckart* (which figures not only as a play but as a 'livre' in Nerval's 'Projet d'œuvres complètes', *NPl 3*, 784–6). His 'translations' are omitted, yet they necessitated no little creative

[8] *NPl 2*, 1696 n.1, 1701 and 1715.

activity on his part: at least as much as it took to copy out certain passages from 'Quintus Aucler' which derive in every particular from Aucler's *La Thréicie*. The question is begged: what, given the restrictive definition of Nerval's work mentioned above, puts 'Le Roi de Bicêtre' into the 'charmed circle' despite its well-known associations with a professional collaborator and its pseudonymous first publication? As an example of the 'moral high ground' to which the *Nouvelle Pléiade* occasionally lays claim, an article by Pierre Enckell in *L'Evénement du jeudi* is typical: 'Et vous pensiez connaître Nerval?' (headline); 'Débarrassé des textes qui lui étaient faussement attribués, des légendes et des interprétations astrologiques qui l'entouraient de fumée'; 'Dégagée des faux problèmes, la valeur littéraire n'en devient que plus pure'; 'Nous avons seulement dégagé les scories et débroussaillé les voies d'accès, pour rendre au texte sa pureté originelle'.[9] Enckell's rather rigid notion of purity contrasts starkly with the limpid poetic purity often assigned to Nerval's use of language. It may seem like a wilful misapprehension to find fault with an editorial policy which is inevitably arbitrary, but prefaces headed 'Nerval, tout Nerval, seulement Nerval' may foster expectations of decisiveness which can never in practice be infallible.

Critical Material in Other Editions

Between the first and latest editions, in which reliability is an important criterion in itself, there are a cohort of others, of course not nearly as numerous as those of other texts such as *Sylvie* or *Aurélia*, that are mainly interesting for the editorial opinions expressed in them in so far as they help trace a history of the possible ways of interpreting the significance and signifying processes of this text.

After Lecou, *Les Illuminés* next appeared as Volume Four of the six-volume Michel Lévy 'Complete Works' of 1867–8, thus becoming the first of the posthumous editions. It contains all the seven pieces published by Lecou, but also an eighth: 'Les Successeurs d'Icare', a reprint of Nerval's preface to Julien Turgan's *Les Ballons* (1851). What it calls *Les Faux-Saulniers* (included after *Les Illuminés* in the same volume) is composed of (i) *Angélique* and (ii) 'L'Histoire de l'abbé de Bucquoy', although the combination of the two does not actually produce the text of the *feuilleton* published in 1850 in *Le National*.[10]

9 *L'Evénement du jeudi* (30 Nov. 1989), 134.

10 See Jacques Bony's notes to *Les Faux Saulniers*, *NPl 2*.

Thus begins a long critical tradition of ascribing incompleteness to the Lecou version of *Les Illuminés*, and so adding one or more texts supposed, on the evidence of a letter to Limayrac of 31 July 1853, to have been intended for inclusion in a second volume. The *Nouvelle Pléiade* justifiably calls the Michel Lévy edition 'un volume qui ne fait pas foi'.[11] Its credibility, in the case of *Les Illuminés*, is not improved by Aristide Marie's mistake in his bibliography, where he appears to amplify 'Le Roi de Bicêtre' of this edition into a 275-page epic, omitting details of the subsequent pieces; and the mistake is copied out by Jean Senelier in his first 'Bibliographie nervalienne' of 1959.[12] In the context of the contention that *Les Illuminés* has been neglected, the misrepresentation perpetuated by Senelier is worthy of note, because it has not been subsequently corrected, although four volumes of the *Bibliographie* were published.[13]

The first significant twentieth-century edition is Marie's *Illuminés* of 1929 (Champion), part of the unfinished *Œuvres complètes* undertaken by Marie, Marsan and Champion. Marie may make some errors, but his general comments are perceptive even though this brand of scholarly writing now shows its age. His Introduction cuts through the intricacies of the Illuminist movement and grasps the more crucial quality of this work as a descriptive collection of eccentrics and almost a second *Praise of Folly*.

Several other editions cluster around this period, the most unusual being that published in two volumes in 1926–7, each with a preface by Henry Frichet.[14] Volume One contains only 'Les Confidences de Nicolas', while its partner boasts, in this order, 'Cazotte', 'Cagliostro', 'Quintus Aucler' and finally 'Le Roi de Bicêtre'. There is no sign of Bucquoy or indeed of Nerval's prefatory uncle. The point need hardly be laboured that this is an entertaining rather than a scholarly publication: Frichet implies that Nerval committed suicide in the

11 'Notice' to *Le Bonheur de la maison*, *NPl 1*, 1616.

12 Aristide Marie, *Bibliographie des œuvres de Nerval* (Paris: Champion, 1926), 19: '*La Bibliothèque de mon oncle*, p. 1–2; *Les Illuminés: le roi de Bicêtre (Raoul Spifame), XVIe siècle*, p. 3–278. *Les Faux Saulniers; I: Angélique. II: Histoire de l'abbé de Bucquoy*, p. 279–471'.

13 See Jean Senelier, *Gérard de Nerval: Essai de bibliographie* (Paris: Nizet, 1959), 64. The state of Nerval's bibliography is alluded to by Bony (*L'Esthétique de Nerval*, 279). Michel Brix's 'Manuel bibliographique des œuvres de Gérard de Nerval', *Etudes nervaliennes et romantiques* 11 (1997), is certainly a welcome addition.

14 *Les Illuminés*, Pages retrouvées (Paris: André Delpeuch, vol. I: 1926; vol. II: 1927).

early hours of Christmas Day 1854, thereby getting not only the month but the year concerned wrong, and shortly afterwards gives the subtitle of *Aurélia* as 'Le Rêve *de* la vie'; 'Weishaupt' is given as 'Weshampt' and 'Quintus Nantius' as 'Quintus Nautius' (Delpeuch edition, 11, 7 and 9 respectively).

Another version, the fifth from a series of nine volumes edited, according to Volume I, by Henri Bachelin, was published by François Bernouard in 1929, in a relatively luxurious format, but this is not an edition generally praised for its exactitude. However, in a critical appendix, Bachelin reprints the interestingly barbed appraisal of *Les Illuminés* by Armand de Pontmartin.

The most reliable edition of this group is one published by Le Divan which, unusually, reproduces the subtitle *Récits et portraits*; it is introduced and edited by Henri Clouard (1927). Again, this forms part of a Complete Works project, although this is not clear from the title pages of the individual volumes. Clouard stresses the unfinished, heterogeneous aspects of the work, and perceives Nerval as engaged in a quest for originality and uniqueness. Quite unlike the assessment of Richer cited earlier, Clouard's introduction portrays 'Jacques Cazotte' as symptomatic of Nerval's need to earn a crust rather than as a fine example of his prose. Many other choices of single parts of *Les Illuminés* for special prominence seem equally arbitrary. Mercure de France's 'Les Plus Belles Pages' series (1905) publishes only 'Cagliostro', an accolade somewhat relativized since, no doubt, by Jean Richer's discovery of its extremely close resemblances to its source text.

The *Ancienne Pléiade*, edited by Béguin and Richer, appends to the Lecou contents of *Les Illuminés* a section, 'Illuminés et Illuminisme', containing parts of *Le Diable rouge: almanach cabalistique pour 1850* generally attributed to Nerval (to which latter the *NPl* editors have added one piece), and 'Textes divers' including such not uninteresting oddments as Nerval's review of the reopening performance at the Diorama (*L'Artiste*, 15 September 1844), and once again 'Les Successeurs d'Icare'. Richer later added a 'Projet de publication' to this *dossier*, one claimed to be by Nerval and to be found among the manuscripts in the Lovenjoul collection pertaining to *Le Diable rouge*. This wide-ranging thematic list, not republished by the *Nouvelle Pléiade*, would seem to confirm Nerval's overriding interest in the supernatural and in unorthodox religious sects and personalities at around the time of *Les Illuminés*—if any authentication were actually available, or any evidence that these articles were more than one day's dream;[15] the posthumously reported account of Nerval's speech to his friends before setting to work on this almanac is a good antidote to taking the 'Projet' too seriously:

> Il n'y a pas encore une ligne d'écrite. On a quatre jours pour mettre *Le Diable rouge* sur ses pieds. Nous allons nous y atteler à deux pour aller plus vite; chacun se chargera d'une jambe [...] Il y a là, dans ce sac, pêle-mêle, les bois autour desquels doit figurer notre prose. Plongeons donc, à tour de rôle, la main dans l'urne, et chacun se chauffera du bois que lui aura fait retirer le sort. (*NPl 1*, 1926)

The previous Pléiade edition of Nerval's works is permanently thrown into doubt by its successor. It is certainly true that it favours mysticism and occult symbol systems unduly as keys to interpreting Nerval—to which the grouping of analogous texts around *Les Illuminés* as evidence of the *necessary* constitution of a second and virtual volume testifies; its scholarly apparatus is not always consistent; and its attributions of a substantial proportion of the texts it claims to have added to the known total of Nerval's output are unsound. Yet its days seem far from numbered, partly because it is simple to consult compared with its successor. There is much logic to the *NPl*'s non-publication of letters addressed *to* Nerval as well as those *by* him, but the partial selection that appears in *APl* can often be helpful. If the version of *Les Illuminés* in *NPl 2* largely supersedes *APl*, it is because Max Milner avoids the excesses of the polemic between the two.

APl was followed closely by a publication of *Les Illuminés* in Garnier's *Œuvres complètes*, Volume I, of 1958 (reprinted in 1967). Its editor, Henri Lemaître, also appends a section 'En marge des Illuminés', as he does for a majority of the well-known mature works, but it is less the critical apparatus of this edition than its measured and undogmatic approach which is its outstanding feature. It too implies that *Les Illuminés* is unfinished, but refrains from any too impressionistic speculation about its possible extensions, and gives a rare mention of the humour present in this text (especially in the story of Bucquoy, parts of which are comparable to *Jacques le Fataliste*).

Another version of 1958 is edited by Monique Cornand, and this Bibliothèque Nationale-sponsored edition systematically glosses all the vocabulary which poses problems for a twentieth-century reader.

[15] *APl 2* (2nd edn., 1961, and subsequent *APl* edns. only), 1215.

Although it aims to reproduce the Lecou edition, it also includes the texts dealing with Leroux, Considérant, Towiansky and Lamennais from *Le Diable rouge*, 'qui auraient pu constituer le début d'un deuxième volume'.[16] It becomes clear that this idea was extremely prevalent at a certain point, since it is common to the last three commentators: but what, in that case, is to be made of a line in the draft 'Bibliothèque de mon oncle' where, writing of 'la vie et le caractère de mes excentriques', Nerval adds the word 'inconnus' (*NPl 2*, 1712)? By the time of the preface's writing, Nerval seems not to intend his work to be encyclopaedic, or to provide more than a subjective choice of figures. Otherwise, Cornand's edition is unremarkable, as is that of Robert Kanters.[17]

In a strange reversal, Jean-Baptiste Baronian's edition of 1973 is subtitled on the *inside* 'Précurseurs du socialisme', while on the cover it is *Les Illuminés: le livre des génies fous*. Although this appendage may show an awareness of Nerval's own draft phrase, 'Livre parfaitement sensé sur des folies' (*NPl 2*, 1712), it also immediately locates this edition in a post-Laing, post-Foucault climate of sympathy and voyeurism about madness, confirmed by the prefatory definition it offers: 'Le terme *illuminé* vise plutôt une personnalité qui n'a presque aucun lien avec ce que l'on a coutume d'appeler le commun des mortels'.[18] Despite the Gothically alluring blurb of the back cover ('cet ouvrage dégage une odeur trouble et envoûtante'), Baronian's own commentary is quite discerning. He would divide the work 'down the middle': the last three figures are 'excentriques' ('Cazotte', 'Cagliostro', 'Quintus Aucler') whereas the first three are merely 'de puissants individualistes' whose lives are not informed by Illuminist principles (5–6). But the implied exclusivity of the term 'excentrique' hardly conforms to the broad use which was made of it at the time Nerval was writing—indeed Champfleury's *Excentriques*, also of 1852, are merely quaint figures whom the *flâneur* would have encountered in a walk round Paris.[19]

The Monaco-based Editions du Rocher version of 1992 contains a

[16] Nerval, *Les Illuminés*, in *Œuvres*, ed. M. Cornand, 7 vols. (Paris: Imprimerie nationale, Nouvelle Librairie de France, 1958–60), vol. 3 (1958 [1959]), 11 n. 1.

[17] Paris: Nouvel Office de l'édition, 1964.

[18] *Les Illuminés: le livre des génies fous*, ed. J.-B. Baronian, Collection Univers secrets (Verviers, Belgium: Bibliothèque Marabout, 1973), 5.

[19] See below under 'Different Eccentrics and Other Libraries'.

preface by Guy Dupré called 'Gérard de Nerval et l'autre histoire'.[20] This is a relatively inexpensive, popularizing edition, and some of the preface's claims are suitably hyperbolic: 'Longtemps gardés sous le boisseau, au profit de *Sylvie* et des *Filles du Feu* d'une part, des *Chimères* et d'*Aurélia* d'autre part, *Les Illuminés* retrouvent leur signification et leur importance, si l'on y voit, en même temps que l'étude de certaines altérations ou transfigurations de la personnalité, une véritable généalogie de l'éthique révolutionnaire' (41). There is very little overt linkage between figures in this equivocal book that could justify this claim, although with the wider context of Nerval's knowledge and preferences the sympathetic reader may well fill in some of the gaps to derive this type of message: but it is equally easy to derive a perfect ambiguity, or an altogether different sense, that reading pleasure is reflected thematically in the serendipitous researches of the bookworm himself seeking out the traces of the past peculiar in the personally estranging present. The Editions du Rocher preface further misleads when it adapts one of Nerval's most famous, and tragic, phrases to fit what it sees as *Les Illuminés'* unequivocal perspective: 'Ne vous mêlez plus les pinceaux, car l'histoire est noire et blanche' (42). Dupré ignores any amendments to textual history or interpretation dependent on the *Nouvelle Pléiade* (1984), despite writing for publication in 1992, retaining the erroneous publication month of November, for instance; and he generally echoes esotericist readings and textual comparators directly inherited from the particular expertise of Jean Richer: for instance, in the mention of *Arcane 17* by Breton, or the supposedly exact link with the avuncular library of Gérard Vassal, whose Masonic credentials are listed. There are also some simple mistakes: *Les Illuminés* is not 'douze ans avant *Aurélia*', and neither is the piece on Raoul Spifame to which Dupré is referring at this point (17). This preface is slightly more successful than Richer's initiated attempts to explain the same information (the mytho-hermetic, cabalistic and similar origins of some of Nerval's source materials), notes the irony of the 'precursors of socialism' subtitle fleetingly, and epitomizes a certain branch of thinking for those who would venture further in this direction. The text itself is reproduced with all the punctuation and other interpretations of the *Ancienne Pléiade*.

[20] *Les Illuminés: ou les précurseurs du socialisme* (Monaco: Editions du Rocher, 1992), 7–44.

The final item in the catalogue of editions is in some ways a beginning: it is the 'user-friendly' Folio version of *Les Illuminés*, first published in 1976, in which Max Milner makes many of the salient points subsequently extended in his editorial comments to the same work in *NPl 2*. It remains the best serious, and imaginative, introduction for the unfamiliar reader. Doubts on Milner's part about the authorship of 'Le Roi de Bicêtre' are, in fact, more plainly voiced in the preface here than in the *Nouvelle Pléiade*:[21] 'Certaines particularités stylistiques—notamment le recours à un humour plus appuyé et plus allègre que celui dont Nerval est coutumier—donnent à penser que c'est bien Maquet qui a tenu la plume' (16). It is also here that Milner places a certain emphasis on the importance of Nerval's own preface, 'La Bibliothèque de mon oncle', whose significance is in permitting the inclusion of the writer and his uncle in the textual margins (26–7), at a time when Nerval is often seen as being in the process of inventing his semi-fictional first-person persona for future use. It is here that many of the critical issues relevant to *Les Illuminés* are posited in their most succinct form.

Overview of Related Critiques

Some of the available materials that give significant attention to *Les Illuminés* take it as a whole, and some treat one piece or a pair exclusively, and these two types are treated separately here: they indicate different ways of reading *Les Illuminés* and different expectations on a number of levels. The transition between the two provides an opportunity to ask whether *Les Illuminés* is to be discerned as singular or plural, a question raised by the grammatical form of the title itself.

A preliminary bibliographical list shows surprisingly few studies giving the work sufficient prominence for it to be named in their title: even Gérald Schaeffer's *Une Double Lecture de Gérard de Nerval*: '*Les Illuminés*' *et* '*Les Filles du Feu*', the most notable book-length interpretation to date, gives it joint 'star billing' with another work; indeed, the symbiotic relationship between the two, on which his entire thesis is founded, may be an indication of the same cautious tendency.

The balance of the material still current, though, is in the form of focused articles, of which only those by Michel Brix, Béatrice Didier, Jacques Latournerie, Anne-Marie Jaton and Guy Dupré take the

[21] (Paris: Gallimard, 1976), 7–29.

whole of *Les Illuminés* as their subject. More numerous, but less relevant to the present reading, are a second group of articles that deal—however well—with only one fragment of the whole work; this includes a contingent whose contributions on *Angélique* apply partly to 'L'Histoire de l'abbé de Bucquoy'. A third and final group, affording insights on this text within much wider studies, includes those by Frank P. Bowman, Bruno Tritsmans (*Ecritures nervaliennes*), Jacques Bony and Michel Zink.

It still remains for a complete translation of *Les Illuminés* into English to be produced: so far the only elements available consist of 'Les Confidences de Nicolas' and 'Jacques Cazotte' in Binder's dissertation and an unsatisfactory rendering of 'Le Roi de Bicêtre' by Margaret Gough dating from 1925.[22]

Gérald Schaeffer's *Double Lecture* is arranged along analogous lines to Gérard Genette's *Seuils*, in taking as subsections each aspect of the reader's apprehension of the text in 'anatomical' order, indicated by his section-titles: 'Description de l'ouvrage'; 'Le sous-titre'; 'Le plan de l'ouvrage'; 'La préface'; 'Le Roi de Bicêtre'; 'L'Histoire de l'abbé de Bucquoy' etc.[23] His study lacks some of the attention to small but trying inaccuracies with which he reproaches Aristide Marie: a reference to Auguste Viatte's *Sources occultes du romantisme* specifies no volume number, although there are two, and this page reference is anyway given incorrectly (13 n. 8). The unexplained advocacy of a return to the first publications in journals for the base text ignores the deliberate amendments carried out upon them by Nerval in preparing the Lecou volume. An immediately striking point, upon which reviewers have commented, is Schaeffer's use of a purely Structuralist notion of structure, so to speak, which dominates his critical insights from the very start of his analysis, in a mode inspired by Léon Cellier.[24] His claims for the overarching importance of the central narratives, 'Les Confidences de Nicolas' (always called 'Restif' by Schaeffer) and 'Jacques Cazotte', come in something of a vacuum and rather detract from subsequent attempts to unite *Les Illuminés*: 'Restif et Cazotte sont les deux seuls véritables *romanciers*, *créateurs*, qui offrent

22 This is referred to in the Senelier bibliography of 1959.

23 Neuchâtel: Baconnière/Payot, 1977. *Les Filles du Feu* is also taken to include *Les Chimères*.

24 See the reviews of Henri Bonnet, *Revue d'histoire littéraire de la France*, 80 (1980), 1, 130–1; Jacques Gaucheron, *Europe*, 604–5 (1979), 243–4; and Norma Rinsler, *French Studies* 34 (1980), 88.

une *œuvre* valable par elle-même' (12). Possibly the most perturbing feature of this study is, however, its apparent lack of any awareness that simple binaries of the type 'astres/hommes', 'subjectif/objectif', 'réel/image', 'même/autre', 'réel/imaginaire', 'esprit/chair', 'adoration lointaine/passion humaine', 'conflit/harmonie' should be the departure point rather than the terminus of any critical dialectic which seeks to account for a complex work, even if these binaries do represent one of the most widespread literary mechanisms of (e.g.) Romanticism. Literary structures and systems are interesting for their subtleties rather than for their inflexibilities. To assert that 'les couples de contradictions tendent vers l'unité d'une opération conçue comme un remodelage du réel' (34) seems to be a property of Schaeffer's reading rather than of the object of his discussion *per se*, and the odd truism surfaces: 'Le jeu multiple des reflets, des images et des types réels provient d'une vision esthétique et métaphysique de l'artiste créateur'; 'Seule l'œuvre d'art [...] peut espérer triompher du temps' (34, 45). Schaeffer's comments on 'L'Histoire de l'abbé de Bucquoy', in particular, seem to have little bearing on the *récit* itself and rely on discussion of related Nervalian texts. Most importantly, Schaeffer's study differs from the aim of the present one in attempting to find a single slot into which the entire work will be made to fit: 'il s'agit de chercher à quel *système général* ces rapports *appartiennent*' (39 n.45, my emphasis). Schaeffer's heavy reliance on the idea that Nerval's work can be classified as a branch of realism is not supported by any clarification as to whether this means the specific literary movement or the more diffuse current usage of the term: in any case, *surnaturalisme* seems much more apt to describe the later and greater style of some of the Romantic generation.[25]

A passage in Schaeffer's lengthy section on Rétif de la Bretonne concentrates on the three Nervalian images of women from 'Les Confidences de Nicolas', and resolves doubles or dyads into triadic

[25] For this concept, see 'Problématique du Romantisme', in vol. 7 ('De Chateaubriand à Baudelaire') of the *Littérature française* series, by M. Milner and C. Pichois (Paris: Arthaud, 1985; rev. edn. 1990), 7–17: 'La poésie française a eu son romantisme, mais après 1840 [...] Alors, Baudelaire écrit ses premiers poèmes [...] Alors, Labrunie devient vraiment Gérard de Nerval [...] Certaines de ces œuvres où sont sensibles une dimension métaphysique, un caractère visionnaire, nous les groupons sous l'appellation de *surnaturalisme*, en utilisant un mot qu'emploient sous cette forme ou avec une variante (supernaturalisme) Nerval, Baudelaire et Victor Hugo' (16).

structures, taking the form of three instances of the intervention of fate or destiny in the life of Nicolas (41–8). Thus the three women-figures of Jeannette Rousseau, Marguerite Pâris and Mme Parangon are identified with the abstractions of fatality and chance (they are three Fates, in fact), so that (for Schaeffer) in this fictional world it is not Nicolas who stamps his mark indelibly on the life of Mme Parangon by raping her, but she who 'vient marquer [...] la destinée de Nicolas' (44). Literature and this woman are jointly responsible for the 'destinée néfaste' of which Nicolas is presented as the victim: 'Mme Parangon, trouvant Nicolas en train de lire *Le Cid*, va participer à l'intrusion de la passion interdite dans la vie' (45). While Nerval's narrative covers the traces of Nicolas's act by refusing to name it ('Comment dire ce qui se passa dans cet instant fugitif comme un rêve?', *NPl 2*, 989), Schaeffer underlines the reality of the 'viol sacrilège' of a 'divinité dans sa plus parfaite image', undoing one of the narrative's most typical erasures, but concentrates on the potential of Nerval's female figures to provide material for discussion of the 'mariage rêvé' and the mythic or divine female, leaving aside a possible discussion of how narrative point of view can reify female victims into culpable idols (48).

Schaeffer emphasizes the significance of Nodier (18, 57–61), and foregrounds the importance of 'La Bibliothèque de mon oncle' (22); and he is almost alone in coming up with a non-psychoanalytical reason for Nerval's *gommage* of Rétif's lewder writings: 'Si Restif lui-même a succombé au mauvais goût et au succès facile des anecdotes scabreuses, Nerval se refuse à exhumer des extravagances pour flatter bassement le lecteur; c'est pourquoi il donne de Restif un portrait singulièrement expurgé de toutes ses descriptions priapiques' (16). This suggestion calls upon ideas of (good) taste as a criterion for literary decision-making which may indeed have played a part in Nerval's thinking; it is arguable whether he was aware of the ideological bases of taste and of documentary accuracy. Tastes have become more, rather than less, important, however, in the matter of the racial observations with which Nerval was confronted in his source material: using an example from 'Les Confidences de Nicolas', Schaeffer highlights the fact that Nerval regularly unites diverse characters through *fictional* mechanisms (as opposed to racial criteria) and does not always concur with the racial system of Rétif (53). Schaeffer comments that 'l'ouvrage transmet, par les documents et non par une aléatoire tradition orale, un message sur deux axes, qui se croisent précisément dans le premier récit: la *poésie* et la *législation*' (34). Although this type of comparison is a frequent one in studies of the ironies of *Les Faux Saulniers* or *Angélique*, it is used by Schaeffer in connection with Raoul Spifame and Vignet, spreading the import of the comparison across several sections of *Les Illuminés*.

Anne-Marie Jaton explicitly connects the 'real' figures with the portraits given by Nerval. In 'Nerval "historien" des *Illuminés*', her attention is unevenly divided amongst the six in defending Nerval from critics who accuse him of simplifying and fictionalizing his subject.[26] Cazotte and Rétif are dealt with in some depth, while Bucquoy and Raoul Spifame are only mentioned in passing, but some attempt is made to mention all the sections. Nerval's reconfiguration of the elements of his encyclopaedic knowledge produces a historiographically eccentric effect, but (Jaton notes) he rarely starts off from erroneous factual positions, as some claim.

Raymond K. Binder's contribution is in the form of an unpublished doctoral dissertation, incorporating two translations accompanied by a short commentary relevant to the entire work.[27] Not surprisingly, the approach shows a heavy *Ancienne Pléiade* influence, with the additional trait of aligning Nerval exclusively with Romanticism and constantly highlighting his influence on the work of André Breton in particular. Like Schaeffer and Jaton, Binder exempts 'Le Roi de Bicêtre' and 'L'Histoire de l'abbé de Bucquoy' from consideration: 'There can be no doubt that Gérard was thoroughly versed in the illuminist tradition, and that he knew that people like the abbé de Bucquoy and Raoul Spifame did not really fit in that classification [...] Nerval shows us no evidence that either the abbé or Spifame had any esoteric interests at all' (5). Binder's disappointment at their lack of esotericism is evident, and the notion of variety of approach, such as reading for linguistic and formal 'fit' rather than allusive promptings, is somewhat lacking. His study does provide an extensive survey of the mystical elements of *Les Illuminés*, and the preliminary information relates outward to the rest of the work from which the two centrally placed narratives are set apart.

[26] In *Lumières et Illuminisme: Actes du colloque international de Cortona* (Oct. 1983), ed. Mario Matucci (Pisa: Pacini Editore, 1984), 29–40.

[27] Raymond K. Binder, '*Restif de la Bretonne* and *Cazotte*: Two Biographies from *Les Illuminés* by Nerval translated into English' (unpublished doctoral dissertation, University of Iowa, 1976). For a summary, see *Dissertations Abstracts International* 37, 5 (1976), 2847A.

Reading any article which states that it will be based on the Michel Lévy version of *Les Illuminés* is guaranteed to be an interesting experience, and indeed Jacques Latournerie's '*Les Illuminés*: Gérard de Nerval et Umberto Eco' is fascinating in a number of ways.[28] The potential of the ideas of Freemasonry and mystic sects to be developed into all-consuming obsessions is exemplified in Eco's book *Foucault's Pendulum*. Latournerie has published several pieces of comparative criticism featuring Nerval, and here he suggests just how close is the resemblance between *Les Illuminés* and *Foucault's Pendulum*, at least on the level of references to Rosicrucianism and to the Freemasons—'de pareilles "affinités électives" ne sauraient être l'effet du hasard', he contends (85). Neither is his choice of edition purely accidental, it seems, since the initial Lecou version (1852) provides a different balance of concerns altogether from the Lévy (1867) edition, and Lecou's first two figures (Spifame and Bucquoy) have very little to do with this argument. As it is, Latournerie can dismiss 'Le Roi de Bicêtre' because Spifame is 'un personnage non historique mais de "composition"', and Bucquoy can be left out because Lévy decided to group it with *Les Faux Saulniers* in a different part of the volume. Similarly, Nerval's portrayal of Rétif's ideas lacks any overt correspondence with Freemasonry or Rosicrucianism in the enthusiastically narrow sense which interests Latournerie. His article concludes with a paragraph which inhabits a different plane altogether from that of the argument he has been expounding, describing the experience of an initiation rite from the point of view of the 'adept'. The literally visionary significance of illumination is brought home—

> Pour la réalisation du grand œuvre, l'adepte doit parcourir le quaternaire évolutif. Parvenu à la station IV, il a le choix soit de retomber dans la matière, soit de parvenir au V. C'est le centre du cercle, l'intersection des branches de la croix inscrite. Là le temps et l'espace s'effacent, s'abolissent les contraires. Participant au regard divin, l'initié embrasse d'un seul coup d'œil tous les horizons. C'est l'illumination. (86)

—but finally, this can only provide a footnote to the study of *Les Illuminés*, since its potential for objective comment on the Nerval–Eco 'coincidence' is undermined on all sides: it does, however, invoke an argument which might be developed further by an 'uninitiated' commentator.

[28] *Cahiers Gérard de Nerval*, 14 (1991), 83–6.

Meanwhile, Béatrice Didier, in 'Révolution et identité dans *Les Illuminés*', provides a very different perspective on the text, touching upon the relationship between autobiography and biography, and finally anchoring her comments to the idea of progressing through *Les Illuminés* aided by a permanent awareness of the 1789 Revolution. The study of historical and biographical elements is thorough. In historical terms, 'La Bibliothèque de mon oncle' and the subtitle 'Précurseurs du socialisme' point inexorably towards a meditation on socialism, but in Didier's biographical terms, *Les Illuminés* is about Nerval's 'drame intérieur': 'Retrouver des précurseurs de sa propre folie, n'est-ce pas lui donner une assise, lui découvrir des ancêtres, des pères, en faire une sagesse?' Both Revolution and madness are aspects of Nerval's make-up from which he cannot escape.[29] Especially in the context of the rhetorical question, 'Que devrait-on faire avant d'écrire?', it is a simple step to conclude that 'Nerval a donc choisi d'écrire, mais pour se délivrer' (8). Didier's concise reading of *Les Illuminés* throws out many fundamental points, but fails to persuade one of the text's interest, its power over the imagination of the reader as well as the writer, or of its being any different from so many others which might be, but are not, *Aurélia*.

'Le livre parfaitement sensé sur des folies' is how Michel Brix, following a phrase in the draft of 'La Bibliothèque de mon oncle', describes *Les Illuminés*.[30] Brix notes Barbey d'Aurevilly's criticism, that one cannot know whether Nerval believes (in) what he recounts: but Barbey's actual question ('Sait-il ou ne sait-il pas? Croit-il ou ne croit-il pas?') has a directly religious point, whereas here Brix's implies a critical concern with narrative irony, rather than solely with nineteenth-century considerations of religious scepticism. Brix concurs with those who, basing themselves on its title and political subtitle, see a yawning divide between the expected and actual contents of *Les Illuminés*. The main link between the figures is 'le côté curieux, bizarre, irrationnel, parfois même dément' of their descriptions. Bucquoy, it is true, does not quite fit the 'mad or immoderate' criteria to which the rest conform—he is 'ni [...] un fou, ni [...] un fripon, ni [...] un libertin' (465)—but the irony of his portrait is similar to that of the others. All share in having had an effect

[29] *Cahiers Gérard de Nerval*, 12 (1989), 2–10 (9).

[30] Michel Brix, '"Les Illuminés" de Nerval, ou le "livre parfaitement sensé sur des folies"', *Studi Francesi* 102 (1990), 464–71.

on intellectual posterity (or at least Nerval presents this as being so), and, having been pronounced different (in their dissent) from their contemporaries, they are replaced in their context, as they are no more foolish, in some ways, than others whose behaviour is held up for comparison (466–7). The biographer and historian in Nerval fight for the upper hand, the historian highlighting what is interesting about the thought of each character, which ultimately prevents negative judgement being passed on the dubious elements of their lives exposed by the biographer, in such a way that, as Barbey complains, passing judgement is in fact rendered impossible: the disapproving narratorial tone of some of Nerval's phraseology pre-empts the reader's own disapproval, and in any case the action of judging the conduct of fellow human beings is problematized: 'Nerval ne réhabilite ses héros qu'en jetant le doute sur tout ce qui les entoure, sur l'histoire de la pensée, sur l'humanité tout entière, sur la faculté des hommes à juger de la conduite de leurs semblables' (469). Finally, though, it is to the biographical links between Nerval and his 'heroes' that Brix returns, and to the judgements passed on Nerval's own eccentricity by his peers. Although Nerval can be ranked alongside his six figures as an eccentric, care should be taken about calling the figures and their author mad ('crier à la folie', 471). Brix thus manages to discuss madness *in* the Nervalian text without having to subscribe to the madness *of* the Nervalian text or its author. This is a discerning microcosm of many of the important points which contribute to the specificity of *Les Illuminés*. It resembles many other critiques in having no strong conclusion to draw: or perhaps it would be too banal to have to point out once more that the text in question is, if not 'parfaitement sensé', at least, for Brix, quite sensible, thus affording the opportunity for 'les pages les plus bouffonnes' to be slyly introduced amongst the rational developments of this or that philosophy.

It seems remarkable that this select cluster of studies represents what can be considered all the significant evidence of detailed attention to *Les Illuminés* read exclusively and as a whole. Its sparseness is counterbalanced by a large body of comment that applies to this Nervalian text as much as it does to those more often cited: the work, for instance, of Michel Jeanneret and Shoshana Felman, as far as the themes of (auto)biography and of the identity of insanity are concerned.[31] But one can also gain the impression of being more familiar with *Les Illuminés* than may actually be the case, so often is it touched upon in passing as secondary evidence for observations based upon works deemed more central. A not unrepresentative example of the type of indirect reference found in general surveys is that of R. E. Jones, in his *Gérard de Nerval*: 'To these [*Filles du Feu*] were added *Angélique*, which is related to Nerval's study of the Abbé de Bucquoy which appeared in *Les Illuminés* [...]'.[32]

This type of comment also epitomizes another tendency, to produce readings that refer to only one of the illuminated figures, although the import of the comment is often directed towards the collection as a whole while returning eventually to the apparent aporia of its inescapable heterogeneity. The very title raises a question: is it/are they singular or plural? This is not merely a matter of grammatical rectitude. It touches, more broadly, upon one of the fundamental characteristics of the collection format: its simultaneously singular and plural perception in the mind of the reader, and of the writer. Even in purely grammatical terms, however, the answer is that it is not possible entirely to exclude the singular or the plural here, a point confirmed by native speakers as well as by the evidence of perfectly standard critical usage. It seems pragmatic to treat *Les Illuminés* as both singular and plural in the wider context of its physical and literary existence, too. *They* are texts concerned with such diverse characters as an obscure sixteenth-century lawyer and the prolific printer-turned-writer Rétif de la Bretonne, and they are written in sometimes greatly differing styles and tones, representing literary production over thirteen years (1839–52), roughly half the writer's career in print. *It* is a transitional work in Nerval's literary career, and it is situated at a turning-point between his earlier output (as a writer of *feuilletons* and of prefaces to anthologies of others' writings) and the depth and power of his later work. Above all, they are bound to be resistant to synthesis and neat systematization. Because of this resistant quality, it seems, instances of piecemeal, partial treatment are carried out more readily than comprehensive expositions and investigations of *Les Illuminés*. This singular or

[31] See Michel Jeanneret, 'Nerval et la biographie impossible', *French Studies* 24 (1970), 127–43, and *La Lettre perdue: écriture et folie dans l'œuvre de Nerval* (Paris: Flammarion, 1978); Shoshana Felman, *La Folie et la chose littéraire* (Paris: Seuil, 1978).

[32] (New York: Twayne, 1976), 97.

selective focus sometimes allows more freedom of interpretation within its smaller scope, although it sometimes seems as if the notion of *Les Illuminés*' intra-textual dimension had not been considered.

Critical studies which refer specifically to 'La Bibliothèque de mon oncle' are: Norma Rinsler, 'Gérard de Nerval and Heinrich Heine', and Martin Zimmermann, 'La Bibliothèque de l'oncle: un motif et ses significations'.[33] Those referring uniquely to 'Le Roi de Bicêtre' are a chapter by Claire Gilbert, in her *Nerval's Double: A Structural Study*; Jean Céard, 'Raoul Spifame, Roi de Bicêtre: Recherches sur un récit de Nerval', already mentioned; Walter Kasell, 'Nerval's Innocent Double: "Le Roi de Bicêtre"'; and Ora Avni's theoretical insights in 'A Bicêtre: Austin, Searle, Nerval'.[34]

Further critical work relevant to 'L'Histoire de l'abbé de Bucquoy' cannot overlook that based on *Angélique* and on *Les Faux Saulniers*: both contain elements related to it. The following are relevant: Susan Dunn's 'Nerval, Transgression and the Amendement Riancey'; Phyllis Zuckerman, 'History, Fiction and Legend in Nerval's *Angélique*'; and Geneviève Mouillaud, 'L'Auteur et l'autre', which deals with the Nervalian 'je' and the layering of textual material 'borrowed' or rewritten.[35] Robert Cassagnau declares his specific interest in *L'Abbé de Bucquoy*, but this turns out to be a reference to the source-text rather than the narrative of the same name in *Les Illuminés*; and the article is in fact devoted to paraphrasing *Angélique*. Jean Roussel, finally, notes familiarly of the illuminated figures, 'Tous ces personnages ont en commun d'avoir une identité incertaine, sur laquelle eux-mêmes s'interrogent, et les autres aussi et bien davantage'.[36]

[33] Norma Rinsler, *Revue de littérature comparée* 33 (1959), 1, 94–102; Martin Zimmermann, *Cahiers Gérard de Nerval* 14 (1991), 55–62.

[34] Claire Gilbert, chapter on Raoul Spifame, in *Nerval's Double: A Structural Study* (University, Mississippi: Romance Monographs Inc., 1979); Céard, *Etudes nervaliennes et romantiques* 3 (1981), 25–50; Kasell, *Stanford French Review* 2 (1978), 1, 39–46; Avni, *Modern Language Notes* 98 (1983), 4, 624–38.

[35] Dunn, *Nineteenth-Century French Studies* 12 (1983–4), 86–95; Zuckerman, *Sub-Stance* 20 (1978), 79–90; Mouillaud, *L'Herne* 37 (1980), 243–56. Further central studies of *Angélique*, some of which refer in passing to 'L'Histoire de l'abbé de Bucquoy', are listed in Jacques Bony's 'Note sur le texte' to the former, *NPl 3*, 1197–8.

[36] Cassagnau, 'Gérard de Nerval bibliophile et les bibliothécaires', *Revue française d'Histoire du Livre* 41 (1983), 367–81; Roussel, 'De Girardin à Nerval: la célébrité des soupers d'Ermenonville', *Œuvres et critiques* 10 (1985), 1, 7–18.

Modern readings of 'Les Confidences de Nicolas' often privilege the psychoanalytic over historical and intentionalist considerations of what it may have been considered permissible to express of Rétif's sexual adventures at the time Nerval was writing. The psychoanalytic focus, used discerningly, can be considerably useful in close reading (for instance of the palimpsest text against its precursor), as H. Girard's methodical study of the 'Sara' episode in Rétif and Nerval shows—it would be of interest if such a detailed comparison were to be continued for similarly close passages in 'Les Confidences de Nicolas'.[37] The monograph within which Girard's study is a type of statistical annexe, published by J. L. Bonnat under the auspices of the Department of Psychology at Nantes, veers between basic psychoanalytic and literary-critical approaches. We have seen that the study by Raymond Binder mentions 'Les Confidences de Nicolas' and 'Cazotte' especially, while attempting to situate them within the framework of *Les Illuminés*. Henry Bouillier's 'Gérard et Nicolas' looks at the scant general knowledge of Rétif's writings in Nerval's time and then sketches a familiar comparison between Nerval and the subject of his third 'biography' (its documentary status being as sound as its sources in the highly embroidered autobiographical writings of Rétif de la Bretonne himself).[38] Both have the same 'manie d'antiquaire'; both traced strange genealogies for themselves, not claiming to be famous men but to be descended from them; there is a common taste for actresses, and so on. But, of course, Nerval has changed the spirit of many of Rétif's writings: the latter makes no very special case out of his passion for an actress amongst his many paramours, overtly describes rape and incestuous practices (which in Rétif's mind are to be preferred, in the name of the genetic 'purity' of his proliferating descendants) and has no hesitations about destroying the admiring distance between himself and his idols by sexual conquest. We would never know from Nerval's account that Rétif was a sexual obsessive: Bouillier is keen to dispel any illusions on this score. The interest here is in the identification of one of Nerval's few fellow writers about Rétif at this time, Pierre Leroux. If Leroux is a significant figure for

[37] See H. Girard, 'document annexe', in J. L. Bonnat, 'Gérard de Nerval: Lecteur et biographe de Nicolas Restif de la Bretonne. Essai sur les modalités de l'auto-analyse et de son élaboration, à travers biographie et autobiographie, du point de vue du *genre* littéraire' (unpublished monograph, Department of Psychology, University of Nantes, 1980), 78–130.

[38] Henry Bouillier, 'Gérard et Nicolas', *Cahiers Gérard de Nerval* 12 (1989), 29–37.

Nerval, and Rétif is significant in the eyes of Leroux, 'l'importance qu'il lui attribue est bien la raison pour laquelle il [Nerval] range Nicolas dans la famille des tenants de l'illuminisme' (31). This is plausible, although it is not confirmed, for instance, in letters, or by specific allusions in 'Les Confidences de Nicolas'. Bouillier ends by noting that Apollinaire, unlike Nerval with his *trianonisation* of Rétif's life in Sacy and persistent edulcorations, had no problems personal or otherwise with Rétif's grosser side, since it is this exactly which is treated in 'Histoire d'une famille vertueuse' in *L'Hérésiarque et Cie*. But this may not be so surprising, given that Apollinaire himself had once written pornography for a living and that he was one of the first cataloguers of the 'Enfer' of the Bibliothèque Nationale. Finally, a section of Jacques Bony's *Récit nervalien* is given over to 'Les Confidences de Nicolas'. Bony notes how assiduously and long Nerval worked on this biography, using primary material consisting of around seventy volumes by Rétif, but essentially, he thinks, using the experience as a dry run for autobiographical writing.[39]

The advantages of segmenting the text into units with an uncontroversial 'identity' have perhaps proved rather convenient, and the procedures and influence of structuralism may also have had a part to play in this segmentation. But *Les Illuminés* of 1852 has a different countenance, in its integrality, from its previously published component parts; and this holds true even if one judges Nerval's textual adjustments to each component while preparing the 1852 volume to have been small. Its whole *is* more than the sum of its parts. It is the whole work, problematic or otherwise, the identity of this work, which provides the general background to interpretation here: from a standard author-analytical perspective, this approach helps revise and refine any understanding of the point Nerval's outstanding, if tragic, career had so far reached; from a more postmodern angle, a text that can be seen as a self-creating nexus of dynamically unstable elements is hardly a bad starting-point for further investigation.

Bony's *Récit nervalien* introduces a third and final category of broader critical references, for, as well as singling out 'Les Confidences de Nicolas' for particular comment, it refers briefly but significantly to *Les Illuminés* as a whole, in the context of more general observations. *Le Récit nervalien* deals with *Les Illuminés* concisely under

[39] 'L'Autobiographie d'un autre', in *Le Récit nervalien: une recherche des formes* (Paris: Corti, 1990), 193–200.

a general heading of 'La Conquête du "je"', where comments on *Les Illuminés* hint at the synthesis that might have been made of its importance in its generic and cultural context, as has been done for the Nervalian narratives that are studied in detail. For Bony, an immediate comparison text is *Les Grotesques* by Gautier, a text whose inspiration (if not writing) he credits to the entire circle of the Petit Cénacle and Doyenné groups: 'Les *Illuminés* de Gérard seront à la "philosophie" ce que les *Grotesques* de Théo étaient à la littérature' (192).[40] Bony's work, here and elsewhere, sets about demonstrating the extent to which Nerval tried and expanded the boundaries of many genres, but especially of the *récit*; his comments on 'Les Confidences de Nicolas' are a microcosm of his finely and extensively argued point, one which, surprisingly, it is still necessary to emphasize: that it is time to 'rendre à Nerval le statut d'écrivain' (15).

Returning Nerval to the status of a charmingly pathetic polymath *malgré lui* may be thought easier. Philippe Muray's *Le Dix-neuvième Siècle à travers les âges* includes a long section, 'Pythagore en gilet rouge (Nerval)', balanced on the perceived significance of *Les Illuminés* in having brought together under one conceptual umbrella illuminism and early socialism, in a stroke of daring if perhaps unconscious originality.[41] The claim of originality relies largely on the juxtaposition achieved by the title and subtitle of the book, as the starting-point for a general discussion of Nerval's encyclopaedic familiarity with esotericism. Muray makes a number of points too daring (or inflationary, depending on one's point of view) to have been made by more mainstream studies of the attitudes of and to the nineteenth century's 'Ecole nécromantique': 'Voilà ce qu'il fait toute sa vie Nerval, au fond: il se constitue un avoir. Un patrimoine. C'est un capitaliste du nécrophile. Il déchaîne l'inflation de ses ancêtres. Avant les banques de données et les banques du sperme, il y a les banques des morts et c'est d'ailleurs la même chose' (402–3). His point seems to be that previous studies of the links between revolutionary activity and utopian political and religious systems have either missed the scandalousness of such links or obscured them in a welter of scholasticism: the epitome of such linkages is that between the mystic

[40] See Théophile Gautier, *Les Grotesques* (1844), a collected volume of essays on neglected 16th- and 17th-century poets (Villon, Théophile de Viau, Scarron). Interest in some of them was indeed rekindled by the attention paid them by the Romantics.

[41] (Paris: Denoël, 1984), 399–425.

Catherine Théot and the fleshing-out of the concept of the 'Etre suprême' in the person of Robespierre, who at first colluded in his own deification, then covered it up ruthlessly and suppressed Théot. The episode is mentioned allusively in 'Cagliostro'. Muray also targets those who, from the first, reacted with surprise to the illuminist-socialist link implied by Nerval's title, as if they were wilfully ignorant: in fact, the surprise stems more from the fact that the content of the volume does not appear fully to support the apparent guarantee of the title and subtitle combined, an appearance which remains the case. Many of Muray's dynamic observations are based on relatively well-known structures. Muray seems to be angry with the timidity of academic criticism for not drawing the type of analogy he portrays as obvious:

> Quand je vous disais que le socialisme est injecté d'occultisme, et l'occultisme rechargé à doses homéopathiques de socialisme! Voilà Nerval en train de nous justifier les grandes subversions idéologiques, les grands séismes, les catastrophes du 20e siècle par la tendre solidarité de l'Etre suprême veillant à ce que nous ne quittions jamais trop longtemps la route bien droite de l'avenir radieux. Qui d'ailleurs n'y croit pas en sourdine? [...]
>
> 'Nous vivons dans notre race et notre race vit en nous.' Cette phrase du si gentil poète d'*Aurélia* a fait un malheur au 20e siècle. Un vrai malheur, dans la réalité, dans les corps. La terre et les morts. [...] La race et le sang. [...] Je ne voudrais pas avoir l'air de faire des amalgames abusifs, mais Nerval *ghost-writer*, de loin, des cultes modernes des ancêtres devenus programmes politiques et volonté d'extermination, c'est ça aussi l'action du 19e siècle sur le siècle suivant. (410)

It might have been hoped, however, that the carnage in human lives caused by totalitarian ideologies in the twentieth century would have incited any thinking person to avoid extravagantly broad analogical interpretations of history and favour the disquieting prospect of real, differentiating analysis.

In 'Les Illuminés ou les précurseurs du socialisme', Guy Dupré echoes (sometimes in the same words) the observations made in his preface to the Editions du Rocher *Illuminés* of the same year, giving a general exposition of the thematics of mystery and mysticism, sects and brotherhoods in a style cognate with his almost exclusive use of now superseded references (Peyrouzet, Breton, Daumal, Durry). The most recent work Dupré cites, which is, precisely, Muray's, actually ironizes upon the portrayal of Nerval as one of the nineteenth century's favourite mystic sons—compare this with Dupré's insistence on calling Nerval 'Le Grand Irrégulier'—but proves useful to Dupré in confirming his own point that Nerval is *the* writer to link illuminism and socialism.[42]

Alongside his group of editions of individual Nerval texts, a second study by Bony, *L'Esthétique de Nerval*, already mentioned, underlines crucial insights for a less specialized readership with the aid of an anthology. It is true to say that the references to illuminism and socialism in *Les Illuminés*' subtitle *probably* trace the influence of the varied company of the 'bohême galante' days at Impasse du Doyenné (Alexandre Weill, Alphonse Esquiros, Fourierists, and Saint-Simonian sympathizers such as Heine and Liszt) (40–2); the fragmentariness of Nerval's clues to his own aesthetic priorities, at least until the late adoption of the '*je* autobiographique' (which probably ought to be qualified as pseudo-autobiographical), their shifting focus and impressionability, should not blind us to their importance (6–8), or to the metatextual status of many references to the domain of writing, literary research and its paraphernalia (8).

Gérard de Nerval: la conquête de soi par l'écriture, by Frank P. Bowman, deals with Nerval's career and writings on a year-by-year basis, and *Les Illuminés* at first seems to warrant little attention, composed as it is of texts which are already dealt with in the years of their original periodical publication. The study as a whole pays exclusive attention to Nerval's writing and career, but it is a less specialized piece than Bowman's well-known work accounting for the diverse and far-reaching links between spiritual and political thought in the eighteenth and nineteenth centuries. Although he contends initially that there is not much to be added about *Les Illuminés* in their 1852 form since it is nearly all reprinted material, Bowman finally observes: 'On ne doit pas considérer cet assemblage comme un simple travail alimentaire, mais plutôt insister sur le fait que, lorsque les textes de Nerval circulent et sont repris sous de nouvelles formes, ils changent de portée et même de genre, imposant, parfois, une nouvelle lecture' (187).

Bruno Tritsmans includes a section, '*Les Illuminés* comme dérive du mythe de l'Artiste', in his *Ecritures nervaliennes*.[43] Placed in the position of last text to be dealt with 'straight', as it were, before a bridging section into the greater challenges of later work, it is none the less seen to contribute to the complex Nervalian figuration of the artist

[42] *L'Infini* 38 (1992), 94–115.

[43] (Tübingen: Gunter Narr, 1993), 31–8

that is one of Tritsmans's main concerns: 'C'est précisément par le fait que tous ces personnages s'efforcent de remédier (diversement) à une coupure historique et de réinstaurer une nouvelle pertinence qu'ils apparaissent comme des figures de l'Artiste. En même temps, ces tentatives sont présentées comme des apories' (33); the figures stand in opposition to established values, and so inform the problematics of the artist, but by 1852 they do so in a self-effacing way: 'comme si le *projet artistique*, qui fondait toute l'œuvre nervalienne, ne pouvait plus se dire, maintenant, que sous une forme marginalisée'; the caveats of 'La Bibliothèque de mon oncle' show that 'ce n'est que sous cette forme banalisée et innocente que le projet politique de jadis reste dicible' (37).

Michel Zink's 'Nerval in the Library, or the Archives of the Soul' concludes, from a reading that includes the story of Bucquoy and 'La Bibliothèque de mon oncle' amongst others, that Nerval is frequently writing about the vicissitudes of research, libraries and archives, in the same sporadically questing spirit that informs his wanderings around the Valois.[44] Zink thinks this interesting to the extent that library research moves Nerval to search into himself; his project for a historical novel, necessitating historical enquiry, in an attempt to earn a living, is displaced *by* this search, as we see in the case of 'l'illustre Brisacier', fragmentarily waved under the nose of Alexandre Dumas, but never to be finished: 'the result is an "impossible" book' (98). This is contrasted with the experience of writing the almost impossible piece about the abbé de Bucquoy, referred to loosely as *Angélique* 'for the sake of brevity', though what Zink (who does not mention the similar close reading in Daniel Sangsue's *Récit excentrique* of the same material) actually paraphrases is contained in *Les Faux Saulniers*. However, Zink makes a point that hits closer to home: 'Soon there will be no more need to visit a library, to give a card to someone working in the stacks and wait with bated breath for someone not to bring you the book you requested. [...] Imagine, if Nerval had had no difficulty finding the *Histoire de l'abbé de Bucquoy*, there would be no *Angélique*' (103). 'In the end Nerval doesn't doubt that the writer, in using the library with a view toward literary creation, is diverting it to a personal and frivolous use for which it was not intended', although it is only his awareness, with vernacular philology newly become a serious academic discipline in his day, that the library

[44] *Representations* 56 (1996), 96–105.

belongs to its librarians that makes his own activity there seem trivial, and 'all the scholarship in the world seems frivolous in the light of his obsessions and the humorous turn he gives them' (104).

It is along these lines that *Les Illuminés* can be seen as figuring Nerval's private library, in relation to which he himself is, of course, the person not bringing us the book we requested. Meantime, while we are working out what this book is, it does display many of the other features that are perennially commented upon: unstable identities, ambivalently subversive ideals, the privileging of obscurity and eccentricity. The whole is increasingly balanced, as the book progresses, on a wilful grasp of the historically significant text which (unlike Nerval's night) is not at all 'noire et blanche' but finally preserves its intentionally eccentric grey areas, hinting at an erudition whose (over)interpretation, whether as manic utopianism or committed esotericism, it leaves to others. My contention is that, if we accept the library's importance for Nervalian textuality and thematics, perhaps as the figure of an intertextual matrix, we are confronted here with a group of biographical fictions that indicate the process of their own inscription into the personal referential landscapes that Nerval, in pleasure or in anxiety, constantly retraces.

CHAPTER 3

❖

Reading Nerval's Library: *Les Illuminés* and the Literature of Eccentricity

The process of literary transformation peculiar to Nerval outstrips flat description—in the same way that the essential characterization of his more poetical and rhythmic prose proves elusive under the yoke of everyday language. In what concerns Nerval's selection of source material on which to perform interpretational surgery, there is no great degree of agreement: is he a historian writing illicit fiction, or a *romancier* embroidering *à tort et à travers* on the accepted histories? Léon Cellier wrote in 1957: 'Sauf le cas particulier où le souci du rare a poussé Nerval à exhumer des documents peu connus, il se contente le plus souvent de puiser à tort et à travers dans des ouvrages de vulgarisation'.[1] Cellier goes on to discriminate (following Durry) between the quality of the source and the quality of the result, but his previous forthrightness persists in the memory, outweighing the later qualification. Auguste Viatte's famously lapidary statement is in similar vein: 'On n'écoutera point sans preuve un romancier tel que Gérard de Nerval: il emprunte une partie de sa documentation à Nodier, on sait ce que vaut la source: à peu près autant que Nerval lui-même; cela n'empêche pas des historiens d'ajouter foi à ses fictions et d'en assimiler la valeur à celle des manuscrits originaux.'[2] The comment is, partly, just—in protesting against using the work of a *littérateur* as reliable documentation. In spirit, however, it is dismissive of both Nerval and Nodier, neither of whom would unironically claim

[1] 'Où en sont les recherches sur Gérard de Nerval?', *Archives des Lettres modernes* 3 (1957), 1–32 (12).

[2] *Les Sources occultes du Romantisme: Illuminisme—Théosophie, 1770–1820*, 2 vols. (Paris: Champion, 1928), i, 11.

academic accuracy for their fictions. With reference to *Les Illuminés*, Nerval is acting more as a creative writer than as a historian of illuminism in any acceptably narrow definition of the term; the semantic field of the word illumination and the broader literature of eccentricity are, ultimately, more enlightening.

Les Illuminés and the History of Illuminism

A number of the names and movements from the history of illuminism in its broadest sense are mentioned in *Les Illuminés*: Nerval does not choose to explain many of them in any depth; in his own time, many of his readers would have been conversant with these movements, but today his litany of names requires an amount of research. This may explain why so much scholarship related to *Les Illuminés* concentrates on the gaps between accepted fact and Nerval's readings.

Auguste Viatte's *Sources occultes du Romantisme* is still, despite its age and angle, one of the most notable sources of information on the ramifications of Illuminism and its intertwined relatives; but his summary dismissal of Nerval is hardly designed to endear him to the partisans of 'le doux Gérard'. A more specific account is found, naturally enough, in Aristide Marie's introduction to his Champion edition of *Les Illuminés*. His colourful *mise-en-scène* with its moments of heightened dramatic interest seems heavily influenced by the narrative historical style of the Romantics themselves, and bristles with the same evocative naming power Nerval's own texts display. Marie refutes Viatte's accusations, partly by denying any possible comparison between Nodier ('sceptique conteur')[3] and the tragic visionary Nerval. A different sort of *somme* is given by Jean Richer's *Gérard de Nerval et les doctrines ésotériques*, and parts of *Nerval: Expérience et création* contribute valuable documentation about these figures, though the unilateral *lecture-clef* Richer propounds makes them less useful to the unconvinced.[4] More recently, Georges Décote's 'Irrationalisme et illuminisme au dix-huitième siècle: Notes bibliographiques' ends with a special mention of Cazotte, whom he considers to have been underestimated; he regrets halfway through his article that 'des études plus nombreuses ont été publiées sur des

[3] Marie, Introduction to his edition of *Les Illuminés*, p. ix.

[4] *Doctrines ésotériques* (Paris: Griffon d'or, 1947); *Expérience et création* (Paris: Hachette, 1963; rev. edn. 1970).

personnages moins intéressants sur le plan intellectuel et qui ne sont guère que des aventuriers', amongst whom he counts Cagliostro and the Comte de St-Germain.[5] In view of the attention Décote pays to Cazotte and Cagliostro (plus another figure of fascination for Nerval, St-Germain), a passing allusion to *Les Illuminés* in this bibliography might have been justified; the article remains a useful beginning on the subject. Anne-Marie Jaton defends the diversity or subjectivity of the choice of *illuminés*, since the disparity amongst them is, as she sees it, a true reflection of the heterogeneous nature of the movement. Jaton treats Nerval as if he were a historian with literary tendencies, but her argument does balance out some of those previously mentioned by taking Nerval's project seriously. Nerval's idea of the *illuminé* as it appears here is historiographically eccentric enough to have provoked criticism and doubt over his intentions: Barbey is the first, but typical, in suggesting that the figures inscribed into what we now know as *Les Illuminés* are insignificant, and that a book intended to represent a typical sample of the eighteenth century's initiates into mystic movements would hardly have left out the Comte de St-Germain;[6] many have since suggested, for broadly similar reasons, that *Les Illuminés* is incomplete.

Such arguments ignore three fundamentals. The title of the collection has potentially ironic value, as does the much discussed subtitle 'précurseurs du socialisme'—nowhere does Nerval guarantee that his sample is typical, and if anything, the contrary is likely. Secondly, elsewhere, for instance in the eleventh letter of *Angélique* (*NPl 3*, 522–3), Nerval is quite capable of discussing *illuminés* in the historically accepted sense, members of Weishaupt's Illuminist sect: 'Les Illuminés français et allemands s'entendaient par des rapports d'affiliation. Les doctrines de Weisshaupt et de Jakob Böhme avaient pénétré, chez nous, dans les anciens pays franks et bourguignons': this contrasts nicely with 'les illuminés qui préparaient silencieusement

[5] *Le Français dans le monde* 49 (1967), 6–11 (10).

[6] An incomplete manuscript called 'Le Comte de St-Germain', whose colourful, descriptive narrative style suggests it might have finished up as a play, is the subject of letters about its publication dated 30 Nov. 1853, well after the appearance in collected form of *Les Illuminés*: its date of composition is not known but is thought likely to be at least two years earlier than this, and so before the publication of *Les Illuminés*: whatever may have prevented Nerval from including it (time? inability to write much through mental distress?), he still went ahead with this project: if St-Germain had been so central, would he have done so? See *NPl 3*, 771–5 and nn., 829, 830.

l'avenir', no capital letter this time, associated with the 'soupers d'Ermenonville', a more various group of visionaries, to whom he alludes a few paragraphs earlier, equally uncontroversially. And thirdly, there is a veritable host of figures whom Nerval does indeed mention, but whose contribution to his subject is transformed into an almost ritualistic recitation of names and works, fragmenting the narrative, in the manner of Nodier's *kyrielles*, into a catalogue.[7] Both 'Cagliostro' and 'Quintus Aucler', situated at the close of the volume, contain references, in more and more telegraphic form, to the balance of the implied contents of the uncle's library. In 'Quintus Aucler', Nerval, sometimes through borrowing from *La Thréicie*, mentions a total of eighty figures or groups, characteristically stretching back to the times of the Old Testament and ancient Egypt, all of whom may have made some contribution to the history of mysticism. Both 'Quintus Aucler' and 'Cagliostro' start, as it were, with a broad sweep through the subject-catalogue of Illuminism, diverting in central sections to the philosophies of the figures concerned and their potential or actual applications, exiting from narrative again by a widening of the viewing angle to a more generalized context; understanding this context depends almost entirely on an intimate knowledge of the signifying power of Nerval's personal mytho-theology. The eccentric effect of the *récits* may be heightened by Nerval's awareness of philosophical correlates and literary intertexts, leading him on a digressive odyssey further and further from the figure in hand:

> Nous avons cité déjà les divers auteurs qui unirent leurs efforts pour fonder en France une doctrine philosophique et religieuse empreinte de ces idées. On peut compter principalement parmi eux le marquis d'Argens, l'auteur des *Lettres cabalistiques*, dom Pernetty, l'auteur du *Dictionnaire mytho-hermétique*; d'Esprémenil, Lavater, Delille de Salle, l'abbé Terrasson, auteur de *Sethos*, Bergasse, Clootz, Court de Gebelin, Fabre d'Olivet, etc.
>
> Il faut lire l'*Histoire du jacobinisme* de l'abbé Barruel, les *Preuves de la conspiration des illuminés* de Robison, et aussi les observations de Mounier sur ces deux ouvrages, pour se former une idée du nombre de personnages célèbres de cette époque qui furent soupçonnés d'avoir fait partie des associations mystiques dont l'influence prépara la Révolution. ('Cagliostro', *NPl 2*, 1132)

[7] See Nodier's *Histoire du roi de Bohême et de ses sept châteaux* (Paris: Delangle, 1830; photographic reprint Paris: Plasma, 1979). A 'kyrielle' is a type of litany.

Les livres traitant de la cabale et des sciences occultes inondaient alors les bibliothèques [...] L'abbé de Villars, dom Pernetty, le marquis d'Argens, popularisaient les mystères de l'*Oedipus Ægyptiacus* et les savantes rêveries des néoplatoniciens de Florence. Pic de La Mirandole et Marsile Ficin renaissaient tout empreints de l'esprit musqué du XVIIIe siècle, dans *Le Comte de Gabalis*, les *Lettres cabalistiques* et autres productions de philosophie transcendante à la portée des salons [...] L'héroïne du *Diable amoureux* n'est autre qu'un de ces lutins bizarres que l'on peut voir décrits à l'article *Incube* ou *Succube*, dans *Le Monde enchanté* de Bekker.[8] ('Jacques Cazotte', *NPl 2*, 1083–4)

But significantly, it seems that Nerval opted to make passing reference to the literary existence of figures such as Martinez Pasqualis and Dom Pernety, rather than write biographies for them. He uses some of the figures whom he does choose to include as a kind of organizational shelf or catalogue drawer where he can, by the evocative power of a cited name, amass the philosophical or other contributions of those whom his critics see as more central.

Semantics: From Illuminism to Illumination

Few encyclopaedia definitions of the Illuminist movement *per se* seem to coincide neatly with what one might extrapolate from the choices of figure made by Nerval: the sect of the *Illuminati* will provide only a temporary and partial signpost into the text and its title—especially for a reading which encompasses perspectives broader than the purely contextual ones, making definitions contemporary with the present as useful as those contemporary with Nerval. *Les Illuminés* has its own language, not of Illuminism but of illumination, denser and more diverse than the thematics of religious mysticism. The terminology associated with Illuminism itself has broadened out of its specialized niche in the years since the work was first published; and, equally, the lexical possibilities offered by illumination are wider, more suggestive, and no less relevant to a poetic reading of this text. Nerval's influence on both of these semantic fields is problematic but detectable.[9]

Defining *illuminé*, Littré gives 'orné d'illuminations' as an older

[8] Nerval consistently misspells some of these names, which I cite in their uncorrected form from the edition indicated.

[9] Gérald Schaeffer (in *Une Double Lecture*) turns to a Bachelard-inspired poetics of fire to interpret *Les Illuminés* before going on to make the evident connections with his second text, *Les Filles du Feu*.

usage than the substantive indicating a religious visionary; the definition of *illuminé* as it is later used is pejorative: 'noms de certains hérétiques qui se prétendaient éclairés de Dieu d'une manière particulière'; under *illuminisme* Littré similarly gives 'Opinions chimériques des illuminés', continuing: 'Particulièrement: l'ensemble des opinions professées vers la fin du dix-huitième siècle par Saint-Martin et Swedenborg'. This 'particular' usage, which actually signifies an increased breadth in meaning, since the influence of Saint-Martin and Swedenborg became so popularized, is first given by the *Dictionnaire de l'Académie* in 1878 (seventh edition, the preceding one dating from 1835); the Academy previously indicated the *illuminé* to be a member of a certain heretical sect or a religious visionary, as Littré does. On the other hand, modern usage-orientated reference works indicate a further slippage or diversification of the accepted meaning towards the secular: the *Petit Robert*, declaring that the word *illuminisme* first appeared in the language in 1819, gives it initially as a mystic movement associated with Swedenborg and Boehme, and instances '*Illuminés et illuminisme* de Nerval', evidently confusing *Les Illuminés* with Jean Richer's *Ancienne Pléiade* collective heading for works loosely connected with the theme.[10] The second *Petit Robert* definition, however, is: '*Psychiatr.* Exaltation pathologique accompagnée de visions de phénomènes surnaturels'—coincidentally or not, an almost exact description (in current terms) of the state of mind displayed by the narrator of *Aurélia*. The Collins-Robert bilingual dictionary bluntly gives the least mystical description of all: '*illuminé*: visionary, crank'. An independent example, in the form of a quotation culled from Villiers de l'Isle-Adam, shows that *his* use of the term already resembles the ostensibly modern ones in referring apparently to a pathological state of mind, while also harking back to beliefs which deny death any permanence:

D'Athol vivait double, en illuminé. Un visage doux et pâle, entrevu comme l'éclair, entre deux clins d'yeux; un faible accord frappé au piano, tout à coup; un baiser qui lui fermait la bouche au moment où il allait parler, des

[10] Richer's assumptions about the unfinished character of *Les Illuminés* led him to include 'Projet de publication', parts of the *Almanach cabalistique*, a review by Nerval of a production of *Le Diable amoureux*, 'Une lithographie mystique' (Napoleon as 'le magistrat du Verbe'), the review of the reopening of the Diorama, 'Le Bœuf gras', 'Les Dieux inconnus' and 'Les Successeurs d'Icare' in his appendix, 'Illuminés et Illuminisme'.

affinités de pensée *féminines* qui s'éveillaient en lui en réponse à ce qu'il disait, un dédoublement de lui-même tel, qu'il se sentait comme en un brouillard fluide, le parfum vertigineusement doux de sa bien-aimée auprès de lui, et, la nuit, entre la veille et le sommeil, des paroles entendues très bas, tout l'avertissait.

Just before this passage, we read: 'Et des phénomènes singuliers se passaient maintenant, où il devenait difficile de distinguer le point où l'imaginaire et le réel étaient identiques'.[11] The latter seems a strange inversion of a potential Nervalian phrase, musing on where to discern the imaginary and the real being identical, rather than not being so; although the critical point must be the same, the perspective is different.

It is tempting to see Nerval's work exerting a direct influence on such evident semantic slippages, though only the *Petit Robert* mentions Nerval, and this is in connection with a definition of illuminism which arose before the nineteenth century.[12] More than anything else, it is probably the late nineteenth and early twentieth centuries' development of the sciences of the mind, plus the success of psychoanalytical and political arguments in transcending and displacing the importance of religious thought, which has laid the ground for such a transformation, redefining both Nerval's *exaltation pathologique* and the opium of the masses in the process.

Illumination is essentially similar to Illuminism and *illuminés* in being associated by lexicographers first with '[une] lumière extraordinaire que Dieu répand dans l'âme d'un homme' and on a human scale with '[une] inspiration subite, lumière soudaine qui se fait dans l'esprit' (both from *Petit Robert*). Otherwise it denotes what is currently thought of as a form of perhaps superfluous ornamentation, although in the terms of the illustrators of the time it would have been unusual to separate *forme* and *fond* in such a manner—'Terme de paléographie. Enluminure, peintures dont on ornait les manuscrits au moyen âge', as Littré has it. In other words, it is not necessarily the dispensable commodity we might think: and figurative language, such as the reference to illumination itself, can be defended in precisely the same

[11] Villiers de l'Isle-Adam, 'Véra', in *Contes cruels* (Paris: Garnier, 1968; first published Paris: Calmann-Lévy, 1883), 22.

[12] Anne-Marie Jaton also supports Nerval's influence on the semantic drift of this word, and regards dictionary references to pathological states as evidence of Nerval's reconfiguration of Illuminism. She dates lexical transformation with questionable precision between 1847 and 1857. See Jaton, 'Nerval "historien" des Illuminés', 31.

manner: 'Such *figures* were long described as primarily "ornaments" of language, but they are entirely integral to the functioning of language, and in fact indispensable not only to poetry but to all modes of discourse'.[13] The *Petit Robert* calls the use of *illumination* in this semantic area a 'sens ancien, repris à l'anglais', and refers to Rimbaud's poetic cycle of the same name. In fact, the development of the two verbs *illuminer* and *enluminer* is almost completely intertwined, both deriving from the Latin *illuminare*.[14] In the earlier recorded vernacular examples, *enluminer* was used both as 'to light up' and 'to decorate', but it became more specialized as a bibliophilic term during the sixteenth century. Meanwhile *illuminer* came into general usage as 'to light up', but examples are also recorded of its occurrence in the book-orientated lexicon, as illustrated by the sixteenth-century example from La Boétie we saw earlier: 'Petits enfans qui, pour voir les luisans images de livres illuminez, apprennent à lire'.[15]

Different Eccentrics and Other Libraries

Nerval's narrative may at times pass through the thematics of sects and doctrines, and may allude to the contributions of illuminated thinkers from pre-Christian times onwards to the contemporary state of political, religious or philosophical thought: but the historiographic plane of *Les Illuminés*, although intellectually seductive, is on another level purely a *point de départ* for Nerval's imagination. His sense of scholarly enquiry and factual grasp are considerable, but he is not a historian, and his findings are put to the service of an unerring sensitivity to the suggestive powers of his own language. This itself is guided by the need, shown more clearly in the later works, to communicate with the consensus whilst remaining aloof from its attempts, epitomized in the imperative use of the language and grammar of rationality, to moderate his claims for the experience of

[13] M. H. Abrams, *A Glossary of Literary Terms*, 4th edn. (New York: Rinehart and Winston, 1981; first published 1941).

[14] W. von Wartburg, *Französisches Etymologisches Wörterbuch*, 14 vols. (various towns and publishers, 1928–61), iv (Basel: Helbing and Lichtenhahn, 1952), 560–1.

[15] See Ch. 1. A 17th-cent. use of *illumineur* as a craftsman confirms this type of use: 'Les maistres peintres, sculpteurs, brodeurs, doreurs et illumineurs de ceste ville d'Amiens'. This is from an act of 14 Sept. 1642 referred to in a work by Augustin Thierry on the *Tiers État*, and listed by Godefroy's *Dictionnaire de l'ancienne langue française (IXe au XVe siècles)*, 10 vols. (Paris: Vieweg, 1881–1902), iv (1885), 543.

insanity by forcing his expression to conform to expectations.

That *Les Illuminés* has eccentricity as its *raison d'être* is very clear: eccentricity, *pour ne pas dire* folly, *not to say* madness—the phrase 'un livre parfaitement sensé sur des folies' occurs in the draft of 'La Bibliothèque de mon oncle' but is significantly absent from the final version (*NPl 2*, 1712).[16] It is a different, but in some ways analogous, affair to argue that the Nervalian library constituted by *Les Illuminés* is erratic, though not so much so as to refer only outwards. Each bibliographical *kyrielle* only echoes another one; the catalogue is a catalogue of cross-references. It is not so much the visionary figures who are eccentric as Nerval's perspective upon them.

Nerval's perspective on his subjects is *calculatedly* different, and what this produces is surprising in comparison with other writing which might be expected to cover some of the same territory. Champfleury's *Les Excentriques*, of the same year, is in two parts: the first has the same title as the entire collection, the second is 'Les Hommes du ruisseau'.[17] 'Les Excentriques' are ten in number, and include 'Jean Journet'. 'Le Musicien Dubois' was replaced by 'Les Communistes de Ste-Croix' for the second edition of 1855: the third edition dates from 1856, indicating how popular this analogue of *Mayhew's London* for Parisians must have been: it is a work whose *parti-pris* realism owes much to the interest in physiognomy in the wake of the recently deceased Balzac and exemplifies a style which may have passed for objective description at the time. The preface, 'A Honoré Daumier', begins:

> N'avez-vous pas rencontré plus d'une fois sur le pavé de Paris des êtres qui s'emparent de votre regard, que vous ne pouvez oublier quand vous les avez vus?
>
> Quelquefois ces personnages n'ont rien de surprenant ni d'étrange dans leur costume; tout est dans leur physionomie, que les utopies, les rêves, les idées ont rendue bizarre. A ce métier, le masque devient étrange, le corps suit la marche de l'esprit. Swedenborg l'a dit en une phrase ineffaçable:
>
> 'L'homme extérieur est moulé sur l'homme intérieur'. (3)

The preface to *Les Illuminés* involves the reader without apostrophizing him or her in this conversational way; Nerval is a user

[16] Michel Brix's article alluding to this phrase does so in order to argue familiarly for the status of all the pieces in the book as part of an 'autobiographie déguisée', but they are more than an anxious and covert self-justification, as this might be taken to imply.

[17] Paris: Michel Lévy, 1852.

of clichés himself, but those he uses are rarely as heavy as that with which Swedenborg is credited by Champfleury. In *Les Illuminés*, relatively little space is devoted to physical characterization (the description of Cazotte comes overtly from Nodier), and equally little for the reifying anatomical dissections practised by Champfleury on his eccentrics, whom he qualifies patronizingly, or perhaps quaintly, as 'rusés-naïfs' and 'drôles'. 'Les véritables excentriques s'ignorent [...]', he writes, 'Ils se déshabillent sans se faire prier, vous avez l'homme nu. Ils enlèvent complaisamment l'épiderme, vous avez l'écorché. Ils font bon marché de leur chair, de leur sang, de leurs veines, vous avez le squelette. / Quand on a bien vu ces drôles qui semblent des pièces artificielles d'anatomie artistement construites [...]' (8, 9). Nerval's scientific phraseology, towards the end of his own preface, associates his *illuminés* with this fashionable jargon: 'Analyser les bigarrures de l'âme humaine, c'est de la physiologie morale,—cela vaut bien un travail de naturaliste, de paléographe, ou d'archéologue' (*NPl 2*, 886), but the 'vaut bien' hides disapproval of realist quasi-scientific procedures, as the evidence of the study of Rétif shows repeatedly: 'On a abusé depuis de ce procédé tout réaliste qui consiste à faire de l'homme lui-même une sorte de sujet anatomique' (*NPl 2*, 956); 'Si loin que nos auteurs modernes poussent le sentiment de la personnalité, ils restent encore bien en arrière de l'amour propre d'un tel écrivain' (*NPl 2*, 995); 'On ne peut pousser plus loin le *réalisme* littéraire' (*NPl 2*, 1041); 'Il est impossible de mieux s'exposer en sujet de pathologie et d'anatomie morale. Et malheur à ceux-là mêmes qui assistaient complaisamment à ce dangereux spectacle!' (*NPl 2*, 995–6); 'Il en est de même de cette école si nombreuse aujourd'hui d'observateurs et d'analystes en sous-ordre qui n'étudient l'esprit humain que par ses côtés infimes ou souffrantes' (*NPl 2*, 1074). The most scathing attack on philanthropic voyeurism associated with realism also includes writers of the *feuilleton-roman*, amongst whom Nerval must still have included himself in 1850: 'Quelle fortune immense il eût fait de notre temps en luttant de vitesse avec nos plus intrépides coureurs du feuilleton, et de fougue triviale avec les plus hardis explorateurs des misères de bas étage!' (*NPl 2*, 1061). Nerval's *Les Illuminés*, then, is probably not designed to be a realist exercise in anatomization; and his later *Nuits d'octobre* attempts to avoid the pitfalls he describes here.

The final paragraph of Champfleury's preface exempts poets from inclusion in his *Excentriques*: 'Les poëtes ne vivent pas selon les lois de la société: ils marchent dans la vie les pieds en l'air, la tête en bas [...] [ils] reçoivent déjà assez de coups de pied des ânes qui les entourent, sans les exposer publiquement en compagnie des presque fous, aux risées d'une foule ignorante' (19–20). In this case, Champfleury must later have de-classified Nerval as one of these exempt poets, since he is posthumously portrayed in another collection, *Grandes Figures d'hier et d'aujourd'hui*, as nothing if not an eccentric, alongside the customary human and animal anecdotes: Gérard attempts to give his hat to a hippo in the Jardin des Plantes; Gérard buys a lobster which he fails to give to Janin and then donates to Méry along with a parrot; Gérard gives a speech proving that he and his friends were 'tous d'anciens perroquets'; the goldfish in the Tuileries pond invite Gérard to dive in as the Queen of Sheba is waiting, which he refuses to do in case it wounds Solomon's vanity. However, Champfleury also sympathizes with the pace of work Nerval may have set himself in order to rival a Dumas or a Balzac: 'Gérard, qui n'a pas beaucoup écrit, a trop écrit encore'.[18] Nerval's work which he or others qualified as realist ('Mes Prisons', *Promenades et Souvenirs*, *Les Nuits d'octobre*) is criticized, since realism should 'montrer un homme'. There is no record of what Champfleury thought of *Les Illuminés*, but a letter shows that he was aware of Nerval's interest in cognate topics, for he wrote to Nerval suggesting a book he might read on the subject of Illuminism: 'Vous devez connaître le livre de Mounier, *De l'influence de la franc-maçonnerie et de l'illuminisme lor* [sic] *de la révolution en France.* / Au cas où vous ne l'auriez pas, j'ai cru qu'il rentrait trop parfaitement dans votre travail futur pour le laisser échapper'.[19]

Philarète Chasles's article on eccentrics in the *Revue des Deux Mondes* dates from 1834, and shows in retrospect how much the term had become 'naturalized' in the twenty-odd years which separate it from Champfleury's book.[20] Chasles starts by defining this strange locution: '*Excentriques* ou gens bizarres de l'Angleterre [...] *Eccentric, eccentricity*, mot emprunté à l'astronomie,—l'ellipse irrégulière des comètes,—une conduite en dehors de toutes les règles reçues, et du système général' (497). His article takes the form of an interview with an English 'eccentric-collector', Wordem, who vaunts the indi-

[18] *Grandes Figures d'hier et d'aujourd'hui* , Œuvres illustrées de Champfleury (Paris: Poulet-Malassis et de Broise, 1861), 220.

[19] See Letter XXXVI, *APl 1*, 972, dated [1851]; Champfleury goes on to give the price and the bookseller where Nerval can buy the volume.

[20] 'Les Excentriques', *Revue des Deux Mondes* (1 Sept. 1834), 497–558.

vidualism of the English with a final flourish which sounds a strangely familiar Eurosceptic note: 'Chez vous *originalité* est synonyme de folie; chez nous c'est un éloge et un honneur. Mais cela finira bientôt. Nos rapports avec le continent nous perdront' (509). Wordem, an architect, then gives the narrator the run of his library, and the following chapters of the article provide a tour. In the final and twenty-third chapter ('Bibliothèque absurde'), we find a Nervalian staple, *Le Songe de Polyphile*, in a list of books nobody has ever understood (556); a character appears who traces his mythical lineage on the basis of rather dubious etymologies, and Sterne and Nodier are mentioned, along with Cazotte ('que vous n'appréciez pas'), as 'vrais humoristes', by contrast with Scarron, whom Wordem at the start of the piece thinks wrongly described as a humorist, for he should be a melancholic.

Chasles's journalistic writing is lighter than Nerval's, and this article is by no means the first or last in a line of 'bibliothèques des fous'. His eccentrics are of all types including highwaymen, and yet his article bears better comparison with *Les Illuminés* than Champfleury's collection simply through its less highly coloured and less infantilizing attitude towards its subject, its sprinkling of real insights and nice ironies. It also shares its thematics of the library with *Les Illuminés*. Another student of the eccentric is Nodier, who apart from his novel, surreal *avant la lettre*, about the king of Bohemia, also wrote *Monsieur Cazotte*, from which some descriptions are cited in the 'Jacques Cazotte' of *Les Illuminés* (*NPl 2*, 1091–2). Nodier, librarian of the Arsenal, played an important role in Nerval's *cénacle* days. His fictions made him no ordinary librarian, and he is one of the few figures in Nerval's work towards whom frank admiration rather than sly irony is directed. The most famous of the many 'bibliothèques des fous' produced by well-known bibliophiles and lexicographers from the 1820s to the 1880s is Nodier's *Bibliographie des fous: De quelques livres excentriques*.[21]

Another is Gustave Brunet's *Les Fous littéraires: essai bibliographique sur la littérature excentrique, les illuminés, visionnaires etc.* The latter mentions Boehme, Jérôme Cardan, Cyrano de Bergerac, Fourier, Jean Journet, La Peyrère (*Pre-Adamitæ*), Leroux, Michelet, Paracelsus, Rétif de la Bretonne, Sade, St-Martin, St-Simon, Swedenborg, Towiansky, and [...] Gérard de Nerval (86–7). Brunet, in his

[21] See bibliography for this and following references.

Dictionnaire des ouvrages anonymes suivi des Supercheries littéraires dévoilées, also produced an 'Essai sur les bibliothèques imaginaires'. The imaginary libraries concerned are nearly all satirical in intent and their paradigm is Rabelais. In the seventeenth century, imaginary catalogues also started to be invented, perhaps to satirize those of entire private libraries sold at auction. The real catalogues provide much evidence, not about reading habits but about the works whose material possession demonstrated an acceptable level of culture in a household, before *cabinets de lecture* and public libraries existed.

Alongside the 'bibliothèques des fous' there are a group of grandparental and avuncular libraries which bear striking similarities to Nerval's. The much longer narrative entitled *La Bibliothèque de mon oncle* by the Swiss Rodolphe Töpffer, first published in 1832, has been broadly studied by Monique Streiff Moretti, who defines the relationships of similarity and difference between it and Nerval's preface.[22] The import of her study is that, although the image of the child in the uncle's library may be inspired in part by Töpffer, his message, that there is an antithesis between erudition and life, is refuted by Nerval, whose citation of the title is therefore ironic. A comparison between Nerval and Heine has highlighted a possible similarity between their uncles' personal libraries: Heine's is also said to have contained mystic objects such as globes and planetary charts, alembics and retorts, and manuscripts relating to astrology and alchemy.[23] The library is in fact a topos in many fictional and semi-fictional writings, and it has been argued that in many instances the 'patrimoine livresque' is actually a 'matrimoine' belonging to the maternal grandfather.[24]

[22] Geneva: Imprimerie de la Bibliothèque universelle, 1832. Monique Streiff Moretti, 'Portraits dans une bibliothèque: Nerval, Töpffer et quelques autres', *Cahiers Gérard de Nerval* 5 (1982), 23–36.

[23] Norma Rinsler, 'Gérard de Nerval and Heinrich Heine', 99. More recently, Martin Zimmermann has refuted some of the claims of this article, maintaining that there is no *relation de dépendance* between the various writers who exploit the theme of the library: 'ils exploitent seulement les virtualités sémantiques du motif', and since Heine is not thematized, there is no reason to suppose that there *is* any connection with him. (In my view, there is also no reason to suppose that there is none.) See 'La Bibliothèque de l'oncle: un motif et ses significations', 60.

[24] Rebecca M. Pauly, *Le Berceau et la bibliothèque: Le Paradoxe de l'écriture autobiographique*, Stanford French and Italian Studies 62 (Saratoga: Anma Libri, 1989): the section 'La Ligne de partage' (3) invents the concept of 'le stade de la bibliothèque' in the child's development.

Thus, the library, as a loosely knit collection, provides *Les Illuminés* with significant intertextual resonances; 'La Bibliothèque de mon oncle' not only suggests an interpenetration between the *illuminés* and these other thematizations of eccentricity and *grotesquerie*, but also suggests its own possibilities as a figure for the organization of the whole of the work. On the other hand, it is also highly unified *with* that text, since it already begins the work of fiction-making, disguising this with the use of the credible first person so readily identified with the absent author, Nerval. Illuminism, similarly, broadens out into the concept of illumination, so that textual allusions to normative history become less important than close metaphorical reading; and it is once again the figure of the library which enables this shift in emphasis to be achieved.

CHAPTER 4

❖

The Library Catches Fire: Reading Proliferation

Une Préface élusive

In the course of this final chapter, the eccentric library thematized by 'La Bibliothèque de mon oncle' is juxtaposed with a selection of other images of the library, and the possibility of using the poetic potential of this image to found a reading of *Les Illuminés* is examined.

'La Bibliothèque de mon oncle' begins in broadly historical and objective mode, justifying itself by referring to a precursor: 'Il n'est pas donné à tout le monde d'écrire l'*Eloge de la folie*'; but by the concluding phrase it has moved on to question the problem of its own writing: 'Que devrait-on faire avant d'écrire?' Although at one level this question is extremely serious, almost despairing, the intense question of a narrator playing Hamlet (to write or not to write), it has a cheerfully ironic side, since writing has patently already taken place though no answer to the question is forthcoming. The question can be read without irony, and indeed lends itself well to a familiar critical 'line': Nerval may have chosen to write as a form of deliverance, but does deliverance lie in writing, in not writing, or in neither?[1] Yet there are many other ways of reading this 'Que devrait-on faire?', for instance as a form of provocation of the reader: 'What if I stop now? What will you do?'; or the library metaphor may be redeemed from the risk of cliché by the charged reference to (*L'Eloge de la*) *folie*: but perhaps it is intended to be a familiar signpost, referring to other familiar metaphors of the eccentric library.

There could be no better embodiment, in a preface, of Flaubert's

[1] See Béatrice Didier, 'Révolution et identité dans *Les Illuminés*', for an example, applied to *Les Illuminés* and to this rhetorical question.

'Ne pas conclure' than this tacit refusal to summarize claims on readers' interest. Rabelais's rumbustiousness is very different from Nervalian persuasion: 'Et maintenant, toussez un coup, buvez-en trois, et oyez ce qui suit', yet there is a message common to both, as Genette's paraphrase of Rabelais reveals: 'Autrement dit: il faut une préface, mais je n'ai plus aucun message préfaciel à vous adresser; voici donc une histoire sans rapport avec la suite.'[2] 'La Bibliothèque de mon oncle' is not unrelated to what follows it, but does not entirely account for it: Nerval's prefatory message suggests the same unwillingness to provide ultimate motivation. It is worth examining the language of these few pages in some detail, and this preface as a whole is sufficiently elliptical to deserve inclusion, with that of Rabelais, in Genette's category of the 'préface élusive'.

Nerval's skill in revising his earlier draft of this piece is evident. In the changes to the manuscript draft, his prose gravitates towards harmonious vowels and smooth rhythms. Comparing what might have been the opening sentence of the preface with what it became, the equilibrium and measured pace of the second are evident, as the phrase

> Il n'est pas donné à tout le monde d'écrire l'*Eloge de la folie* mais sans être Erasme, Fontenelle ou Voltaire, on peut prendre plaisir à nettoyer d'anciennes médailles ignorées ou frustes, à restaurer des toiles d'une composition bizarre dont la peinture éraillée fait sourire l'amateur moderne. (*NPl 2*, 1711)

becomes

> Il n'est pas donné à tout le monde d'écrire l'*Eloge de la folie*; mais sans être Erasme,—ou Saint-Evremond, on peut prendre plaisir à tirer du fouillis des siècles quelque figure singulière qu'on s'efforcera de rhabiller ingénieusement,—à restaurer de vieilles toiles, dont la composition bizarre et la peinture éraillée font sourire l'amateur vulgaire. (*NPl 2*, 885)

The stylistic turns of this final version, in terms of the balance and weight of concessions building to a strikingly rhythmic, and yet ambiguous, finish, are on a par with one of the most memorable of all Nerval's phrases: 'Telles sont les chimères qui charment et égarent au matin de la vie. J'ai essayé de les fixer sans beaucoup d'ordre, mais bien des cœurs me comprendront' (*Sylvie*).[3]

[2] Gérard Genette, *Seuils* (Paris: Seuil, 1987), 158. Genette's quotation is from Rabelais's *Quart Livre*.

[3] In *The Order of Mimesis*, Christopher Prendergast's reading of this phrase finds it

Daniel Sangsue links the stylistic concessives in the writing of *Angélique* (such as 'Je ne sais pas si tout le monde prendrait le même intérêt que moi à dérouler ces pages terribles', 'Pardon de ces minces détails') to Jeanneret's category of 'textes qui relèvent d'une maîtrise de la folie' (*La Lettre perdue*), and notes that 'on est tenté de voir [...] quelque chose qui relèverait d'une *compulsion de défense.* [...] A l'évidence, le narrateur s'efforce de prendre des distances, comme s'il cherchait à exorciser quelque chose d'inquiétant'.[4] Sangsue's section is headed 'Figures du trouble', and both the writing tactics and their analysis confirm the evidence of the first phrase of 'La Bibliothèque de mon oncle'. The repeated use of such phrases as 'à un moment où', 'à l'époque', 'dans ce temps-ci' (all *NPl 2*, 886) is noticeable, and apparently seeks to situate these pieces in a chronologically normative framework in which they will be acceptable as historico-biographical sketches. However, the narrator is quick to acknowledge that the figures may seem no more than marginal: 'L'histoire du XVIIIe siècle pouvait sans doute se passer de cette annotation' (*NPl 2*, 886); 'on peut prendre plaisir à tirer du fouillis des siècles quelque figure singulière [...] à restaurer de vieilles toiles, dont la composition bizarre et la peinture éraillée font sourire l'amateur vulgaire' (*NPl 2*, 885). Both the desire to situate the pieces chronologically and the apparent admission of marginality must be read as deliberately submissive tactics.

And yet, these appeasements are undermined elsewhere in *Les Illuminés*, whether it is in the zest with which each figure is attended to (with the possible exception of Rétif de la Bretonne, arguably the most well-known, least marginal figure), or in the work of even the prefatory piece itself to blur the boundaries of time. Contradictory phraseology works to subvert the conventional tense-relations now established, in the phrase 'Une certaine tendance au mysticisme, à *un moment où* la religion officielle *n'existait plus*, avait sans doute guidé mon parent dans le choix de ces sortes d'écrits' (*NPl 2*, 885; my emphasis); normally there would be a forced grammatical separation between 'n'existait plus' (an absolute statement reflecting what must have been presented at the time as an irreversible situation), and 'un

self-consciously clichéd and therefore highly ironic in intent. It is unclear to me whether or not this is verifiable, but it is refreshingly novel. (*The Order of Mimesis: Balzac, Stendhal, Nerval, Flaubert* (Cambridge: Cambridge University Press, 1986).)

4 'Propositions pour une lecture d'*Angélique*', *Lendemains* 33 (1984), 20–31 (25).

moment où', which implies a finite period. Nerval's apparent acquiescences to syntactic and thematic expectations are not what they seem: these practices reveal Nerval's *enjeu*, his crucial need to portray the passage of time (and of those caught up in it) in a consensually acceptable way, whilst keeping it also within his private domain, where language *will* mean what he wants it to, rather than what the consensus demands: 'La question de l'autorité demandera comment le texte définit et établit son "intérêt" pour l'autre; la question de la séduction demandera par quel(s) moyen(s) le texte entend *recruter cet autre* (ainsi construit par le texte) à un programme narratif "oppositionnel"'.[5]

Apart from the relatively covert features above, a number of appeals attempt openly, as might be expected in a preface, to produce a sympathetic reaction in the reader to this book. It is possible that Nerval also sought here a sympathetic response more generally to his own public persona, in which, as he was more than aware, proximity to mental disturbance was viewed as a detrimental phenomenon, rather than, as he would have had it, a source of enlightenment. In the well-polished phrase already cited, the reader is involved in what is presented as a pleasurable process—'on peut prendre plaisir à tirer du fouillis des siècles quelque figure singulière [...] à restaurer de vieilles toiles'—in contrast to which the ambivalent smiling reaction of the 'amateur vulgaire' is implied to be a less important, less intelligent response to the figures Nerval has chosen to include in his book. Although 'vulgaire' does not automatically have pejorative connotations, the entire phrase, coming at the end of the first sentence of 'La Bibliothèque de mon oncle', immediately situates the reader as the writer's 'partner' in the quasi-archaeological process of unearthing unconventional characters.

While the initial images of the restoration of old canvases and rediscovery of material from the 'fouillis des siècles' foreground a rationalizing, analytical reaction to the remnants of past centuries, this reaction is soon transformed into a more urgent, overwhelming one—articulated around the increasingly personal involvement of the writer in rescuing the source matter from oblivion. During this transformation, the 'on' which was earlier apparently used as a device

[5] Ross Chambers, 'Récits d'aliénés, récits aliénés: Nerval et John Perceval', *Poétique* 53 (1983), 72–90 (75: my emphasis): see also 'habiter l'espace de l'autre sans le posséder' (73, citing Michel de Certeau).

by which to involve the acquiescing reader in the pleasure of discovery seems radically to change its implications until its final appearance as the impersonal pronoun of the last sentence. Yet this impersonal pronoun now seems to refer to the narrating persona, and forms part of an agonized question to which, it is implied, there can be no answer: 'Que devrait-on faire avant d'écrire?' (*NPl 2*, 886).

However, of all the statements that go to make up the preface—and they may seem as disjointed as the texts—the ironic comment which may contain the greatest fund of potential meanings refers, albeit in a plural which attempts to minimize its implications, to madness: 'N'y a-t-il pas quelque chose de raisonnable à tirer même des folies! ne fût-ce que pour se préserver de croire nouveau ce qui est très ancien' (*NPl 2*, 886). We note that the question is not followed by its corresponding punctuation but by an exclamation, urgently persuasive. The subordinate clause reaffirms that Nerval's portrayal of time coincides hardly at all with a realistically intended one. As numerous commentators have noticed, Nerval's conception and representation of time are such that 'ce qui est très ancien' actually exists in parallel with what is believed to be new, so that he is gently sarcastic about the gulf which conventionally separates ancient times from the present. Whether the workings of Nerval's time are so removed from the familiar idea of measurable, unilinear time as to be thought 'insane' is a matter for debate. However, when the subject of madness is raised a second time, depriving the first passing reference to it (in connection with Erasmus's *Praise of Folly*) of its contingency, the irony of the tone is a Romantic irony, in that its target is unstable and cannot be located.[6] Nerval consistently presents his own 'folies' as a form of enlightenment from which much more can be gained than the 'sensible' conclusions about time and history to which he appears to allude. The past somehow does not cease to be, it exists in some relation to the equally elusive present which is neither 'behind' nor 'finished' but surrounding and constantly renewed: 'A l'exemple de l'illuminé lui-même, nous avons uni d'un trait l'avenir et le passé', maintains Nerval in the fourth part of 'Jacques Cazotte' (*NPl 2*, 1100).

[6] For this concept of Romantic irony, see (e.g.) Lilian R. Furst, *Fictions of Romantic Irony in European Narrative 1760–1857* (London: Macmillan, 1984).

Ironic Fictions

It has already been observed that the title of the collection may be ironic. In 'A Alexandre Dumas', whilst again evoking earlier writers as part of his library of references, Nerval uses the word *illuminé* in a way which provides a further clue to his own ambiguous intentions in wielding it:

> Du moment que j'avais cru saisir la série de toutes mes existences antérieures, il ne m'en coûtait pas plus d'avoir été prince, roi, mage, génie et même Dieu, la chaîne était brisée et marquait les heures pour des minutes. Ce serait le songe de Scipion, la vision du Tasse ou *La Divine Comédie* du Dante, si j'étais parvenu à concentrer mes souvenirs en un chef-d'œuvre. Renonçant désormais à la renommée d'inspiré, d'illuminé ou de prophète, je n'ai à vous offrir que ce que vous appelez si justement des théories impossibles, un *livre infaisable*, dont voici le premier chapitre [...] (*NPl 3*, 451)

In its defiant irony, Nerval's flourishing of an unwritable book based on impossible theories actually parallels his unanswerable question at the end of 'La Bibliothèque de mon oncle'. In the present case, he seeks acceptance of his 'rational' talents as a writer of the impossible and is prepared to forgo the visionary status of the *fou inspiré* which was to be attached to him anyway, as he probably knew: defeat and ironic triumph are simultaneously present in this passage. If it is read as entirely defeatist, then Nerval's projects, at least in future, must be curtailed: 'faire *l'Eloge de la folie* sans risquer de se faire prendre pour un fou, écrire sur *les excentriques* sans passer pour un ex-centrique [...] Renoncer à un type d'écriture où "manque" un sujet central, où la digression est la règle'.[7] Sarah Kofman contends that only in *Angélique* can Nerval allow himself to imitate the ludic follies of Sterne, Swift and Rabelais. But 'La Bibliothèque de mon oncle' is playful: it recognizes the risks inherent in writing about marginal figures, sketches a defence—'N'y a-t-il pas quelque chose de raisonnable à tirer même des folies!'—and concludes by implying that there is, in any case, no safeguard against this type of reaction: what (else) must one do, Nerval asks, before launching into the act of writing? The 'type d'écriture où la digression est la règle' is characteristic of much of *Les Illuminés*, as we have just seen: the central focus of 'Cagliostro' is a female initiation rite in which the eponymous charlatan takes a

[7] Sarah Kofman, *Nerval: Le Charme de la répétition* (Lausanne: L'Age d'Homme, 1979), 21.

crucial but only fleeting part; 'Quintus Aucler' is at times merely a proliferating series of lists. These digressions differ from those of *Angélique* mainly in their relative lack of self-conscious irony; however, irony is certainly a distinguishing feature of 'L'Histoire de l'abbé de Bucquoy', underlined by leaps in the narrative chronology and point of view. As Bony notes, in connection with the lives of Cazotte and Rétif: 'la volonté de rompre la chronologie du récit et par conséquent de porter atteinte à sa logique, au sens rationnel du terme, de s'en prendre à ce qui est, selon Roland Barthes, "le ressort de l'activité narrative", est l'un des traits les plus marquants des récits nervaliens des dernières années'.[8]

Ultimately, 'La Bibliothèque de mon oncle' remains elusive: the expectation might be that its *discours préfaciel* would orchestrate the clash of realities, mediate between the worlds of the reader and of the text, by playing on the theme of Illuminism itself. It does everything but this; instead it maintains a poetic distance from banal autobiographical scene-setting by producing an imaginative *version* of this procedure. Starting several times from a number of different points which would confer validation on the text—literary predecessors, modern relevance, sources in childhood, scientific enquiries, the desire to complete what has been started—each time it is sucked into a vacuum, paragraphs trailing off after a few sentences, until finally it hits a paradox which spells out a kind of quiet defiance. Meanwhile, it plants the germ of a parallel question in the reader's mind: 'Que devrait-on faire avant de lire? Avant *dé-lire*?'

Worlds of the Library

Eco's *Name of the Rose* provides an informal but undeniably informed expression of the tantalizing perspectives afforded by the *mise en abyme* of the library inside a book inside a library. 'Until then I had thought each book spoke of the things, human or divine, that lie outside books. Now I realized that not infrequently books speak of books: it is as if they spoke among themselves. In the light of this reflection, the library seemed all the more disturbing to me.'[9] If correlations can only

[8] Jacques Bony, *L'Esthétique de Nerval*, 143, citing Barthes's 'Introduction à l'analyse structurale des récits', in *Communications* 8 (1966; reprinted Paris: Seuil, 1981).

[9] Umberto Eco, *The Name of the Rose*, trans. William Weaver (London: Martin Secker and Warburg, 1983), 286. First published in Italian 1980.

tentatively be asserted between the book and the world, between text and context, the only certainty is, perhaps, that each book implies the existence of others; and the critical image of the library carries with it paradoxical and satisfying notions of the undiscovered territory that can be discerned in the confines of books and libraries. It was blasphemous for Eco's monks to set too much store by the contents of the library: its access was forbidden to them and they lived outside it. Borges, on the other hand, in his parabolic *Library of Babel*, creates a narrator whose existence unfurls entirely inside a universal library, which he believes to have no limits, though it does seem to have a door: 'In the entrance way hangs a mirror, which faithfully duplicates appearances. People are in the habit of inferring from this mirror that the Library is not infinite (if it really were, why this illusory duplication?); I prefer to dream that the polished surfaces feign and promise infinity'.[10] A similar antithesis arises in considering the relationship between 'La Bibliothèque de mon oncle' and the rest of *Les Illuminés*: the fictional biographies of the six figures seem separate from the 'Bibliothèque', whose tone is apparently biographical, but they may all be part of the same all-consuming bibliognostic universe.

So much can be gleaned from the suggestive economy of 'La Bibliothèque de mon oncle' that it cannot be read exclusively as a source of biographical evidence, or as a beginning of Nerval's never-to-be-written autobiography, though it prefigures his fully developed autobiographical mode. First-person narrative is used here for the only time in *Les Illuminés*: but any prefatory statement writing 'I' into the text ought clearly to be treated with caution, or at least with an eye to potential ironies.

Along a notional scale of fact-fiction, this preface lies much closer to the fictions which follow it than to autobiography: a fiction in which Nerval is enabled, as narrating 'I', to become the seventh eccentric. Michel Brix hints at this self-encoding, but has recourse to

[10] In *Ficciones*, translated by Anthony Kerrigan (London: Weidenfeld and Nicolson, 1962), 79–88 (79). First published in Spanish 1956. Philippe Destruel significantly connects this Borgesian text with one by Nerval in '*Angélique* et la Bibliothèque de Babel', *Romantisme* 48 (1985), 21–32, but without extending the connection to *Les Illuminés*, and so, briefly, does Michel Zink in 'Nerval in the Library'. For a wide-ranging discussion of the representation of the library in literature, see (e.g.) Anne-Marie Chaintreau and Renée Lemaître, *Drôles de bibliothèques: Le Thème de la bibliothèque dans la littérature et le cinéma* (Paris: Editions du Cercle de la Librairie, 1990).

biography as a foundation for his assertions: 'Nerval établit des liens biographiques précis entre ses héros et lui. Autre Quintus Aucler, l'oncle de l'auteur tendait au mysticisme [...]; il avait formé une bibliothèque où le jeune Gérard découvrit ces "*excentriques* de la philosophie"'; the biographical evidence for this is, in fact, sketchy.[11] Monique Streiff Moretti asserts that Nerval is exercising his 'art d'accommoder les restes' in putting *Les Illuminés* together: the only common denominator between one *récit* and another written up to twelve years later is Nerval's interest in each figure, 'de sorte que le mince avant-propos intitulé "La Bibliothèque de mon oncle" peut, en dehors de toute vérification biographique, être considéré comme fragment d'une autobiographie en construction'.[12] Each of Nerval's works seems linked with others to a more or less intimate extent—but rarely are *Les Illuminés* used as a focal point against which other fragments are juxtaposed: they are themselves seen as the mobile fragments which can be drawn away into different works such as this imagined 'autobiographie en construction'. The various elements of *Les Illuminés* do not *only* belong to some other Nervalian project, continually elsewhere (anywhere out of *Les Illuminés*?).

Nerval is poetically, as much as autobiographically, implicated in his preface. If we are tempted to interpret his *discours préfaciel* here as being of the same order as that of the *récits*, part of the same poetic, this may signal the increasing chronological gap perceivable between *Les Illuminés* and the present day, since we are told that, as a general rule, 'avec le temps, et en perdant sa fonction pragmatique d'origine, le paratexte, sauf disparition, se "textualise" et s'intègre à l'œuvre'.[13] The library of *Les Illuminés* is both a public and a private space, depending on its function. 'La Bibliothèque de mon oncle', whose prefatory statements make up in shifting intensity what they lack in coherence, sets up the theme of eccentric figures, declaring them first to be worthy of interest and later to be no more than footnotes in the history of the eighteenth century.

Installed in Dr Blanche's clinic in Passy, Nerval's narrating persona speaks of the asylum as a refuge in which he can amass all his creative raw material:

[11] Michel Brix, '"Les Illuminés" de Nerval', 469. Norma Rinsler comments on why it is preferable to see the uncle's library as symbolic rather than real ('Nerval and Heine', 99–100).

[12] Monique Streiff Moretti, 'Portraits dans une bibliothèque', 23.

[13] Genette, *Seuils*, 164.

Ma chambre est à l'extrémité d'un corridor habité d'un côté par les fous, et de l'autre par les domestiques de la maison [...]

J'ai trouvé là tous les débris de mes diverses fortunes, les restes confus de plusieurs mobiliers dispersés ou revendus depuis vingt ans. C'est un capharnaüm comme celui du docteur Faust. Une table antique à trépied aux têtes d'aigle, une console soutenue par un sphinx ailé, une commode du XVIIe siècle, une bibliothèque du XVIIIe, un lit du même temps [...] Je me suis plu pendant quelques jours à ranger tout cela, à créer dans la mansarde étroite un ensemble bizarre qui tient du palais et de la chaumière, et qui résume assez bien mon existence errante. [...]

Mes livres, amas bizarre de la science de tous les temps, histoire, voyages, religions, cabale, astrologie, à réjouir les ombres de Pic de La Mirandole, du sage Meursius et de Nicolas de Cusa,—la tour de Babel en deux cents volumes,—on m'avait laissé tout cela! Il y avait de quoi rendre fou un sage; tâchons qu'il y ait aussi de quoi rendre sage un fou. (*Aurélia*, Seconde partie, VI)[14]

The description of the room, with its significant objects and books that trigger his creativity via the filter of memory, suggests that the healing but carceral function of the surroundings is overlaid by the desire to create a space of study and consultation—be it the consultation of memory rather than of physically more cumbersome research tools—in other words, to create a library.

The asylum and the prison as architectural spaces feature strongly in Nerval's work, and undeniably reveal the anxiety and desire predicated in almost equal measure upon enclosure. The evidence provided by *Les Illuminés*, however, does not always reinforce the cardinal locations of theatre and prison or asylum in their position of unquestioned dominance. The topology of the library and within it of the book, the page and language itself, is discernible as a different type of space, less threatening than the prison-asylum but equally mysterious, informing a complex of meanings and textual events. Despite the thematized presence of prisons, theatres and madhouses in this text, the confining and intensifying power of the fictional text itself finds its most expressive paradigm here in the image of the

[14] *NPl 3*, 742–3. Gérald Schaeffer cites this passage and compares the mystical and dilapidated qualities of Nerval's possessions with the uncle's amassed library, also relegated to an attic. His concern is, however, to highlight once again the Nervalian theme of parallel existence in separate worlds: 'un arrangement d'objets et une collection d'ouvrages incarnent le double voyage accompli par Nerval, à travers le monde réel et dans l'univers des songes' (21).

library, giving a different means of access to this text, freeing our readings from the claustrophobia of the prison and the theatre.

Both of these last have in any case already been intelligently investigated, in the case of imprisonment by Victor Brombert in *La Prison romantique.* He mentions 'L'Histoire de l'abbé de Bucquoy' because of its central focus on the Bastille and escape from it (although the narrative is associated by Brombert with *Angélique* and *Les Faux Saulniers*, not with *Les Illuminés*).[15] Any enclosed space is a potential metaphor, or analogue, of prison, and almost any argument may be justified which discovers the ill-concealed anxiety beneath the pleasure or ironic wit in Nerval's tone as he describes themes of enclosure: Brombert discerns fear of imprisonment and asserts that it is born of the association with the claustration of the insane.[16] His scheme thus includes theatres as metaphorical prisons: 'Mais l'image récurrente la plus curieuse est celle du théâtre—alliant les notions de fermeture et d'évasion, barrières et ouverture, voiles et déchirement, plaisir et inquiétude' (133).

It is true that Raoul Spifame's pantomimic audience with his king-double, glimpsed in his mirror, is a poignant moment of farce, and the daring escapes of Bucquoy and the female initiation ceremony in 'Cagliostro' lend themselves perfectly to theatrical comparisons, as do the hyperbolically numerous 'love' scenes from the life of Nicolas Rétif. Nevertheless, in comparison with the taxonomic systems Brombert proposes, *Les Illuminés* is an untypical Nervalian text in that, although it provides thematized theatrical scenes, far fewer of them seem to resonate, to form motifs, than is the case in *Le Voyage en Orient*, *Sylvie* or the *Roman tragique.*[17] In the opening to 'Les Confidences de Nicolas', the young adult Nicolas, not long arrived in Paris, admires his favourite actress, Mlle Guéant, from the distance of the auditorium; the resonances with the opening scene of the later

[15] Whenever, similarly, the topos of the library in Nerval comes under critical scrutiny, the focus seems almost exclusively to be placed on the 'real' Bibliothèque Nationale and other Parisian libraries of *Angélique.*

[16] Victor Brombert, *La Prison romantique: essai sur l'imaginaire* (Paris: Corti, 1975), 131.

[17] In the latter, see e.g.: 'On ne se perce pas le cœur avec une épée de comédie, on n'imite pas le cuisinier Vatel, on n'essaie pas de parodier les héros de romans, quand on est un héros de tragédie: et je prends tous nos camarades à témoin qu'un tel trépas est impossible à mettre en scène un peu noblement' (*NPl 1*, 702). *Le Roman tragique* is extracted in *NPl* from its former sole inclusion in the preface of *Les Filles du Feu*; it was first published in *L'Artiste* in 1844.

Sylvie are evident. Such episodes are, however, punctuations in the mainly uninterrupted narrative flow of *Les Illuminés*.

More than a theatre, for Nerval's Monsieur Nicolas, the city is a tempting blank page on which he inscribes not only initials but details of his other amorous conquests.

> Nicolas avait encore une pensée: c'était de faire voir à Sara les pierres du quai sur lesquelles il avait gravé le chiffre mystique: AD. AD. (Adeline adorée), à l'époque où il venait dans ces lieux mêmes exhaler les plaintes d'un amour sans espoir. Tout était changé. Les deux amants gravèrent tour à tour sous ces chiffres à demi effacés les initiales réelles de leurs noms, et ne quittèrent l'île qu'après avoir vu le soleil descendu derrière les tours énormes du Petit Châtelet. Ils remontèrent par la place Maubert, la rue Saint-Séverin, la rue Saint-André-des-Arcs, et celle de la Comédie [...] (*NPl 2*, 1024–5)[18]

Progressively, Nicolas covers the apparently infinite page of the city with 'chiffres mystiques', and just as his cataloguing activities lead him to create a calendar in which every day of the year is associated with the name of one of his conquests, so he uses the graphic possibilities of Paris's architecture to turn it into a library consisting solely of texts he has written, a Paris where almost any woman he meets may be the daughter of one of his previous unions. Nerval's interpretation of Rétif's life blurs the very clear echoes between literary creation and procreation present in Rétif's own autobiographical writings.

While the theatre may not be extensively thematized in *Les Illuminés*, the same is not true of the prison-asylum. Bicêtre, the archetype of this institution, holds a prominent place in *Les Illuminés*: the story of Raoul Spifame is not the only one to mention this prison-asylum, in whose confines the *aliénés* are kept in their place, the place of marginalization.[19] Although the liberation of the insane from Bicêtre by Pinel at the time of the Revolution marks a break between the eighteenth and nineteenth centuries' types of confinement of the mentally ill, the name of this particular institution did not lose its associated connotations in the French public's mind, just as Bedlam survives in English. Bicêtre's signifying presence as part of the architecture of madness is not, however, the only representation in

[18] Nerval conserves the etymologically correct orthography of what is now 'rue St-André des Arts'.

[19] In 'Les Confidences de Nicolas', Bicêtre's connotations as doom-laden threshold are given a different twist, as Nicolas's antipathetic brother Thomas is a *précepteur des jansénistes* there (*NPl 2*, 961).

Les Illuminés of the containment of madness. Its correlate is the containment of eccentricity within the shelves of a library. Nerval, who as we have seen writes in the first person only in the preface, sets himself up rather as the librarian of 'ces *excentriques* de la philosophie' than as the keeper of the insane.

The Library Illuminated: Documents, Catalogues

It is no surprise that such a library should prove to be an irregular space of eccentricity, a private place, rather than mimicking the centralized panoptical structures of the institutional library. In 'La Bibliothèque de mon oncle', the uncle's library is situated in a liminal space: it is both a preliminary text to the studies of the six *illuminés*, and situates the library in an eccentric geographical position, 'en province', compared with the centrality of the capital. Even if it were admissible to locate the model for this library by linking the uncle-figure to the real great-uncle with whom Nerval lived in Mortefontaine until he was 6, the classic city-dweller's mention of *la province* puts the library in inescapable limbo, somewhere and yet nowhere, into the margins. It is not the geographical but the temporal slippage between episodes which enables the difference between Paris and not-Paris, between eccentric and real libraries, to be blurred, just as 'l'épanchement du songe dans la vie réelle' blurs the two terms of dream and real life. In other Nervalian texts, libraries which really exist(ed) figure more prominently, especially in the ironically frantic search for the 'documentary proof' of Bucquoy's existence afforded by Mme Dunoyer's fictional account: thus in *Angélique*, the *bibliothèques* Mazarine, de l'Arsenal and Richelieu are all searched for clues.[20] However, it is the semi-mythical 'Bibliothèque d'Alexandrie', providing yet another diversionary episode, which seems to bear the greatest resemblance to the library of *Les Illuminés*.

The library as an enclosing space may seem a weaker image than those of the prison-asylum and the theatre already discussed. Egress from the library is less problematic than access, and it is an apparently less exciting locus for creativity than the theatre—being associable less

[20] Again, Philippe Destruel's '*Angélique* et la Bibliothèque de Babel' elicits many of the points of interest inherent in this aspect of *Angélique*. However, Ross Chambers in 1969 explicitly leaves out discussion of the same topic because he perceives it as having already received ample critical attention. See *Gérard de Nerval et la poétique du voyage* (Paris: Corti, 1969), 172–3.

with the passage from real to ideal, as Victor Brombert would have it, than with the otiose details of arranging documents and extracting 'objective' truths from the serried volumes of infinitely extending knowledge. However, the library's silence is not to be equated with peace and stasis, for there is a constant struggle between containment and proliferation which, in some cases, may lead to conflagration:

> The library, a concrete visible structure, begins when the scattered documents housed under its roof are recaptured and organized according to a dream of unity imposed by a rigidly ordered catalogue and are consumed in silence and solitude. Gradually, as the ever-larger masses of documents threaten to expand beyond human control, the librarian counters with ever more rigid structuring systems. Yet, eventually the place that was to serve as a repository of all knowledge, by the very fact of its existence comes to proclaim the inevitable failure of attempts to gather and organize the scattered documents of human production. [...] The captive books overwhelm the captors. As the library becomes less accessible, it also becomes more fear-provoking, and that which was an essential part of the sociopolitical structure becomes a threat to structure. One kind of consumption suggests another; the library is burned.[21]

In this sense, every library that becomes a monolithic structure is potentially open to the same fate as the library of Alexandria. But this is not the end of the story, for there will always be more classification, more knowledge to be revealed, documented and concealed from those without the key to some repository, as Borges, Eco, and here Nerval, suggest. 'Another opaque, windowless structure is built, the masses of documents begin to gather again, the librarian blindly submits himself to the delirium of a catalogue that proliferates toward infinity' (Castillo, viii).

Nerval's uncle's library is not burned, since its threatening significance is neutralized by the uncle's act of abandoning it to the damp and vermin in the attic, but it does not disintegrate totally before the child unwittingly becomes fascinated with it, and in the end attempts to replicate it (shades of Pauly's 'stade de la bibliothèque'?). Nerval's language implicitly acknowledges that the library cannot in fact exclude its obverse, the *bibliothèque de Babel* of the madhouse, although his phrase attempts to reconcile reason with

[21] Debra A. Castillo, *The Translated World: A Postmodern Tour of Libraries in Literature* (Tallahassee: Florida State University Press [1984]), pp. vii–viii. Castillo's debt to the thinking of Foucault is evident from this passage.

'folies', made apparently less significant by being referred to in the devaluing plural: 'Et puis, n'y a-t-il pas quelque chose de raisonnable à tirer même des *folies*! ne fût-ce que pour se préserver de croire nouveau ce qui est très ancien'.

The library having room for eccentricity but ostensibly founded on principles of sanity is a construct which Nerval cannot utterly dissociate, then, from its obverse, the madhouse with its given, imposed rule. Knowledge and insanity are not mutually exclusive. The 'translated world' of literature, in Castillo's term, encapsulates both: 'in the attraction by madness, the world of reason and stilled forms becomes involved in a continual metamorphosis; the scientific space unfolds, breaks into fragments, and is dispersed [...] It is this multiplication of meaning, this excess of false learning [...] that becomes a weight bearing down on the librarian, catapulting him from knowledge into dream and madness' (45). The *librarian* must be taken here to signify 'classifier, organizer, person in whom logic dominates imagination', and any writer, including Nerval, will have evident differences from this figure. However, Nerval's and the librarians' experiences coincide in the tipping over of their burgeoning knowledge into madness.

It is part of the Nervalian textual *folie* (here and elsewhere) to lose focus, to lose individual identity in favour of totalizing knowledge, diversion into different topics, historical comparisons, literary analogues: everything is included, for nothing can be excluded, if the Other and its risky capacity for difference is to be neutralized. Yet this means that the Same is found, or replicated, everywhere, fragmenting and becoming inimical to the very possibility of identity: the double is frightening, precisely because it is the self in a previously unsuspected, and perhaps irrecuperable, form. Shoshana Felman sees the Nervalian tragedy as residing in 'cette perte de l'autre: ce cercle vicieux de l'imaginaire—engrenage narcissique—[qui] constitue le noyau même de sa folie'.[22] 'Je suis l'Autre': Nerval loses the boundaries of himself, his text, and his surroundings, by attempting continually to incorporate more and more parallel religions, more and more esoteric knowledge, into his repertoire-library (hence the 'catalogues' detailing so many esoteric thinkers), at the same time resisting the attempts of the consensus to label him as Other and unreachable, by seducing his reader into a sympathetic point of view

[22] Shoshana Felman, *La Folie et la chose littéraire* (Paris: Seuil, 1978), 74.

and by making madness something other than the utterly unknowable by writing his experience of it.[23]

The desire for reading which can become all-consuming finds apt expression in Bucquoy's admonition, 'Gardez-vous [...] d'un homme qui n'a qu'un livre dans sa poche' (*NPl 2*, 944), balanced by the threatening aspect of this passion from 'Jacques Cazotte': 'Rappelez-vous le mot: *Et scientia eorum perdet eos*' (*NPl 2*, 1108). It has already been seen that in 'La Bibliothèque de mon oncle', Nerval inscribing himself as a seventh *illuminé*, uses the expression 'se *dé-livrer* de ce qui charge et qui embarrasse l'esprit', invoking escape even from the dissolved bounds of the all-consuming self and the expanding library. Foucault, in 'Naissance de l'asile', states that 'L'asile ne sanctionne plus la culpabilité du fou, c'est vrai; mais il fait plus, il l'organise; il l'organise pour le fou comme conscience de soi, et rapport non réciproque au gardien; il l'organise pour l'homme raisonnable comme conscience de l'autre';[24] and, as noted above, the 'given' nature of the asylum's organization echoes and undermines the apparently less arbitrary ordering principles of the monolithic library. Equating Foucault's 'fou' with Nerval's literary personality, momentarily, the latter's 'conscience de soi' leads to no confrontational resolution: he is not permanently incarcerated in Blanche's clinic; exit from the library is unproblematic, it is access which is restricted; and the city does not hem him in. So there are, if anything, too few *voies sans issue*, too many means of escape. *Les Illuminés* is a comparatively 'reasonable' work, but it shares in what I would term Nervalian textual *folie*; *Les Illuminés* has, for instance, a considerable capacity, especially in the latter portraits of Cagliostro and Quintus Aucler, for tangentiality and ellipsis. It is here that the eccentric catalogue takes off under its own seductive energy, and creates out of these pieces hybrid forms, part bio-bibliographical document, part discursive essay, part narrative fiction too.

In the work of any other writer, literary form might have provided yet another possibly immovable obstacle forcing a confrontation. For Nerval, though, form is sometimes respected (in the sonnet forms of *Les Chimères*, for instance) but the possibility of its being illusory

[23] Ross Chambers's excellent 'Récits d'aliénés, récits aliénés' is a central essay for understanding the narrative techniques involved in these processes.

[24] Michel Foucault, *Folie et Déraison: histoire de la folie à l'âge classique* (Paris: Plon, 1961), 582–3.

eventually encourages it to be undermined. The palimpsestic architectures of Nerval's narrative forms are similarly constructed over the abysses left by his interpretations of the documents he gleans from the historian-librarians: it is hardly surprising that a major reaction to *Les Illuminés* of these people's real counterparts is to detail its historical inaccuracies, departures from the known. Nerval escapes from the constraining obstacle of the expected unity of the work of art via his continual self-palimpsest, to which the indissociable triad of *Les Faux Saulniers*, *Angélique* and 'L'Histoire de l'abbé de Bucquoy' testifies.

It becomes increasingly clear, therefore, that *Les Illuminés* acts as an anti-document and an anti-library, in a reactively subversive sense. In both 'Le Roi de Bicêtre' and 'L'Histoire de l'abbé de Bucquoy', narrative leaks into the lacunae left by libraries and archives: Jacques Bony taxes Nerval with 'contaminating' fact with invention by putting certain prisoners together in the Bastille whose stays there did not coincide, adding that in any case it is impossible to have a full picture of the inmates at the period in which Bucquoy's story is set because the Bastille catalogues register 'd'importantes lacunes pour ces années'.[25] The intercommunicating complex formed by the trio of texts above is a labyrinthine web of pastoral description and anecdotal bibliographical annotation, enmeshed with threads of fact and punctuated strategically with the phrase 'ce n'est pas un roman'. The whole is, intentionally, a nightmare for any librarian, scholar, archivist or bibliophile. Nerval's text connotes its difference from factual scholarship by denoting its attempts to conform to the same normative standard. The final irony is that at the periods of which and at which Nerval was writing, the Bibliothèque Nationale had had virtually no inventory of its holdings since 1720, and so could not produce for him the copy of the text he sought with laconic desperation and which it already possessed (*NPl 2*, 7 n. 6). The situation in which the library found itself was no doubt compounded by the flood of published material, which in the nineteenth century increased vastly: 'le XIXe siècle doit faire face à une véritable prolifération des livres [...] qui donne à certains contemporains (Nodier, Nerval, Balzac [...]) le sentiment préborgésien que leur époque est aux prises avec une Bibliothèque de Babel'.[26]

[25] *Les Faux Saulniers*, *NPl 2*, 151 n.1.

[26] Daniel Sangsue, 'Démesures du livre', *Romantisme* 69 (1990), 43–59 (43).

The tone of the narration gives away its sympathetic attitude towards anti-documentary activity, towards a different species of library governed by a logic not of control but of the gradual liberation of clandestine, revolutionary and philosophically threatening material. Raoul Spifame's 'biography' achieves this by underlining the efficacy of Raoul's forged edicts which prove their success by being, even if indirectly, enacted. They include an edict ordering a copy of every book produced to be lodged in the King's library, the predecessor of a copyright library law. So the author of 'Le Roi de Bicêtre' is materially affected by the preceding activities of the figure he is fixing and possessing via his narrative fiction, since he is bound by the law to deposit one copy of this legislating fiction in the institution which Raoul himself created. The ironic impotence of Spifame and Vignet has in turn been ironized. In 'L'Histoire de l'abbé de Bucquoy', the transgressions of many of the Bastille's inmates parallel those of Raoul—as a 'diagnosed' madman, however, and at this time in the history of madness, Raoul inspires awe and respect, even from his king-double; a later figure who 'avait contrefait les ordonnances du roi' is criminalized because of being judged sane (*NPl 2*, 933).

Thus, proscribed and transgressive texts, as anti-documents, are the stuff of the private library of *Les Illuminés*, which, finally, better resembles the higgledy-piggledy 'capharnaüm' Nerval sets up in the asylum than an orderly, clockwork universe. In 'L'Histoire de l'abbé de Bucquoy', proscribed books have not only a revolutionary but a monetary value: the Protean figure of the salt-smuggling 'capitaine Roland' is also a bookseller: '"Qui est-ce qui cultive? [...] On se bat, on chasse, on fait un peu de faux saulnage [...]; on introduit des marchandises d'Allemagne et d'Angleterre, on vend des livres prohibés. Ceux qui ont de l'argent spéculent sur les bons des fermes; mais la culture, c'est un travail de fainéants!" Archambault comprenait l'ironie de ce discours' (*NPl 2*, 906). In a subsequent chapter, Bucquoy is himself found to be in possession of 'des livres qui ne traitaient que de révolutions', as well as 'un masque et quantité de *petits bonnets*, et de plus encore des tablettes toutes chiffrées' (908). In 'Jacques Cazotte', the text again highlights a brush with authority which takes written material as subversive fact, in this case, real political plotting rather than theoretical incitement, while the narration takes the view that the material may only represent the fictions of at best a fantasist and at worst a victim of senile delusions (in the midst of the revolutionary events of 1791, Cazotte's letters to his friend Ponteau are intercepted, along with other compromising plans to restore the monarchy). Nerval uses his characteristic association of day-dreaming and dream during sleep to attract readerly sympathy for the one unproblematically visionary figure of the six: 'On comprend après tout qu'une pièce pareille ait été jugée fort coupable par le gouvernement révolutionnaire; mais il est fâcheux que l'on ne l'ait pas rapprochée de l'écrit suivant daté de la même époque, et qui aurait montré qu'il ne fallait guère tenir plus de compte des *rêveries* que des rêves de l'infortuné vieillard' (*NPl 2*, 1109). Only *this* personal library could find such an obvious point of community between Cazotte, Bucquoy and mad monarch Spifame—via the misinterpretation of documents whose factual content is not doubted enough.

Rétif is an apparently zealous documenter, especially in his own eyes, of every event which befalls him and which he can narrate for the moral betterment of his readership. He seems unlike Nerval in his meticulous attachment to specific contours of his physical environment. Nerval's craft, on the contrary, enables his narratives to move around the unstable contours of time, rendering even the most familiar topographies mysterious and unfathomable, shattering them into the different moments of their existence. Rétif's documentation, however, betrays that Nervalian over-determination, the same sense of the catalogue consisting entirely of cross-references. His infinitely narcissistic descriptions of sexual and literary triumph in adversity form an encyclopaedia which indicates the Unreason of infinitely reasoning humanity. Paris is a blank page for Nicolas, who gradually, via his graffiti, turns its architecture into a library, and its female population into his family tree.[27]

'Le Comte de St-Germain', the beginning of a potential biography of the eponymous count, was prepared for publication some time after *Les Illuminés* had appeared, as we have seen. Here, Monsieur Rocias the embalmer arrives to find that his 'customer' is alive, having been certified dead by the local doctor. That death certificate is another problematic document to add to the catalogue of anti-documents, which also includes the edicts promulgated by the King of Bicêtre and the conspiratorial papers which help to obtain the convictions of Jacques Cazotte and Bucquoy: convictions which the narrative throws

[27] On the city as library, see parts of Mary Ann Caws (ed.), *City Images: Perspectives from Literature, Philosophy and Film* (New York: Gordon and Breach, 1991).

into serious doubt, as it does the stability and reliability of the documents supporting them.

These documents are, inevitably for a writer of fictions and teller of tales, anti-documents: Nerval may assert the equivalent value of his work with the 'travail de naturaliste, de paléographe ou d'archéologue' in his preface, but his library is of a different order, an avowedly personal one he portrays as a legacy of his own past, rather than the past of the political historian-librarians. Archaeologists are only too willing to concede that their discipline, at least, works from an *incomplete* record. It is clear from the terms of writerly engagement with the 'figures singulières' that history will be rewritten and the past created—'restaurer de vieilles toiles', 'rhabiller des figures singulières' (*NPl 2*, 885). These herald an individual's subjective act of construction which is close to mythography.

Both asylum and prison have metaphorical dimensions suggesting a textual activity of *mise en scène* and incarceration—language dramatizes and imprisons. However, language also holds and reveals secrets, offers the possibility of a consultation of the past embedded in its present. In other words, if language may figure and be figured as a place where secrets are stored and consultation takes place, it is, as well as a theatre and an asylum, a library.

Finally, it is the private library which forms the most effective backdrop to the illicit knowledge we can gain from *Les Illuminés*, knowledge which enlightens Nerval's work as a whole. The library consisting of biographies is, as Nerval writes in connection with Rétif, 'un miroir où chacun peut s'étudier' (*NPl 2*, 1038). For the library, in Nerval's time, is the new locus of revelation, or of illumination: Michel Foucault discusses exactly this kind of imagined library with reference to Flaubert's *La Tentation de St Antoine*, and notes the library's new significance as a place of the imagination in the mind of nineteenth-century writers. 'Le chimérique désormais naît de la surface noire et blanche des signes imprimés, du volume fermé et poussiéreux qui s'ouvre sur un envol de mots oubliés; il se déploie soigneusement dans la bibliothèque assourdie, avec ses colonnes de livres, ses titres alignés et ses rayons qui la ferment de toutes parts, mais bâillent de l'autre côté sur des mondes impossibles'.[28] The library,

[28] Michel Foucault, 'Un "Fantastique" de la bibliothèque', *Cahiers Renaud-Barrault* 59 (1967), 7–30 (10). Reprinted as 'La Bibliothèque fantastique' in Gérard Genette and Tzvetan Todorov (eds.), *Travail de Flaubert* (Paris: Seuil, 1983), 103–22.

while in a sense a place of containment or constraint like the public asylum or the private room in *Aurélia*, is more than this to the imagination; it is, as the apparently rigid divides between each biography in *Les Illuminés* are, a 'structure poreuse'.[29]

In the twentieth century, *Les Illuminés* has often been read as confirming a picture of Nerval the dissenting initiate into occult knowledge, or for its degree of fit with historicity and historical accuracy. But how much of a determining role can these criteria be allowed to play in assessing what is, after all, a work of literature? Orientate the floating fictions of Nerval's *illuminés* around fixed sources and we imply that a merely passive form of creativity was being elucidated, subject to the historical justifications of the Amendement Riancey satirized in *Les Faux Saulniers*. In biographical terms, the writer was at a turning point in his career and moving increasingly towards an exclusive focus on independent, imaginative writing: a third type of interpretation foregrounds the degree to which, again, this text is more significant for what lies in another sphere: Nerval's investigation of his own situation and his need (as it has been perceived) to find an autobiographical 'voice', here through the life stories of others. This cannot be the end of the list of available interpretative strategies. Nerval's contemporaries were inclined to read *Les Illuminés* within the spectrum of what they called the novel, and we can take our cue from them by according it some of the privileges of a work of imaginative fiction, by investigating its spirit of generic challenge or conformism, and by taking into account its playful textures. The inventions detectable on and below the textual 'surface', its slips and incongruities, its figurative qualities, everything should alert us to the possibility that its own inscriptions of problematic identity are prolonged into our relationship with its very dynamics.

[29] Michel Jeanneret, *La Lettre perdue*, 227, referring to *Octavie*.

APPENDICES

❖

Appendix 1: The Individual *Récits*

(a) Individual publication prior to inclusion in Les Illuminés

'La Bibliothèque de mon oncle' :
[MS: Lovenjoul collection, D.741, folios 115–17.]

'Le Roi de Bicêtre' :
(i) *La Presse*, 17–18 September 1839.
(ii) *Revue pittoresque*, 1845.

'L'Histoire de l'abbé de Bucquoy' :
Le National, 7–22 December 1850 (as part of *Les Faux Saulniers*).

'Les Confidences de Nicolas' :
Revue des Deux Mondes, 15 August, 1 and 15 September 1850.[1]

'Jacques Cazotte' :
(i) parts in *L'Artiste*, 20 April and 11 May 1845.
(ii) parts in *La Sylphide*, 29 June 1845.
(iii) as preface to *Le Diable amoureux* (Ganivet, 1845).[2]
(iv) parts in *L'Almanach prophétique pittoresque et utile pour 1847* [Aubert, November 1846].

[1] Also announced in *La Semaine littéraire du courrier des Etats-Unis* (New York, 11 Nov. 1851).

[2] *Le Diable amoureux* was published in 30 instalments. The publication was in association with the *Revue pittoresque*. The articles under (i), (ii) and (iv) are not printed or mentioned in *NPl 1* in their chronological place, where they fit thematically with Nerval's huge journalistic output of the period, perhaps because they are nearly identical to what was eventually published in *Les Illuminés*.

'Cagliostro' :
Le Diable rouge. Almanach cabalistique pour 1850 (Aubert, 1850 [October 1849]): chh. 1, 2, 3 and 5.

'Quintus Aucler' :
Revue de Paris, November 1851.

(b) Chronological order of appearance in print of these versions

(Small roman numerals in parentheses refer to versions of each text indicated in the table preceding.)

September 1839	'Le Roi de Bicêtre'
1845	'Le Roi de Bicêtre' (republished)
April, May, June, November 1845	'Jacques Cazotte' (i, ii, iii, iv)
October 1849	'Cagliostro'
August, September 1850	'Les Confidences de Nicolas' (i)
December 1850	'L'Histoire de l'abbé de Bucquoy'
November 1851	'Les Confidences de Nicolas' (ii)
November 1851	'Quintus Aucler'
May 1852	*Les Illuminés*, including 'La Bibliothèque de mon oncle'

Appendix 2: Source Materials for *Les Illuminés*

'La Bibliothèque de mon oncle'
- No isolated sources.

'Le Roi de Bicêtre'
- Secousse, 'Mémoire', in *Histoire de l'Académie royale des Inscriptions et Belles-Lettres*, XXIII (Paris: Imprimerie royale, 1756), 271–7.
- *Biographie Michaud.*

'Histoire de l'abbé de Bucquoy'
- [Anne-Marguerite Petit, Dame Dunoyer], *Evénement des plus rares, ou Histoire du Sieur abbé comte de Buquoy* [*sic*], 2e édition, ([no place of publication], 1719).
- Madame C*** [Anne-Marguerite Petit, dame Dunoyer], 'Histoire de l'abé de Buquoit', in *Lettres historiques et galantes de deux dames de condition, dont l'une étoit à Paris et l'autre en province. Ouvrage curieux*, 3e édition, 5 vols. (Cologne: Pierre Marteau, 1710–12), v (1712), 25–45.

'Les Confidences de Nicolas'
Numerous of Rétif de la Bretonne's works, including:
- *Le Paysan perverti*, 4 vols. (Paris: published by the author, 1775).
- *Monsieur Nicolas, ou le cœur humain dévoilé*, 17 vols. (Paris: published by the author, 1796–7).[1]

'Jacques Cazotte'
- Jacques Cazotte, *Le Diable amoureux* (Naples [Paris]: Lejay, 1772).
- Jacques Cazotte, *Œuvres badines et morales, historiques et philosophiques*, 4 vols. (Paris: J.-F. Bastien, 1816–17).[2] (*Le Diable amoureux* is included in vol. 1.)
- Mme d'Hautefeuille, 'La Famille Cazotte', in *Le Correspondant*, 1845. Also published under the pseudonym 'Anna-Marie' in one volume in 1846.
- Jean-François de la Harpe, *Prédiction de Cazotte, faite en 1788 et rapportée par La Harpe* (Paris: Les Marchands de nouveautés, 1817).

[1] For a modern edition, see the 6-volume 1959 edition (Paris: Pauvert), or the 2-volume 1989 edition by Pierre Testud. [2] Reprinted in New York in 1965.

'Cagliostro'

• La Roche du Maine, Marquis de Luchet, *Mémoires authentiques pour servir à l'histoire du comte de Cagliostro* ([no place of publication], 1785).

'Quintus Aucler'

• Q. Nantius Aucler, *La Thréicie, ou la seule voie des sciences divines et humaines, du culte vrai et de la morale* (Paris: Moutardier, an VII [1798–9]).

Appendix 3: Contemporary Reviews of *Les Illuminés* (in chronological order of appearance)

Gautier, Théophile, 'Gymnase: Représentation de Mme Volnys', *La Presse* (24 May 1852), 2.

Prémaray, Jules de, 'Les Livres', *La Patrie* (6 July 1852), 4.

Goncourt, Edmond and Jules de, '*Les Illuminés*', *L'Eclair* (10 July 1852), 8–9.[1]

Asselineau, Charles, '*Les Illuminés, ou les précurseurs du socialisme*', *L'Athenæum français* (28 August 1852), 132–3.

Bell, Georges, 'Revue bibliographique', *Mercure de France* (1 September 1852), 639–45 (640–1).

Lewes, G. H. 'Contemporary Literature of France', *Westminster and Foreign Review* (1 October 1852), 614–30 (629).

Barbey d'Aurevilly, Jules, 'Bibliographie', *Le Pays*, 21 March 1853, 3.[2]

Limayrac, Paulin, 'Feuilleton de *La Presse*: Livres: Gérard de Nerval', *La Presse* (31 July 1853), 1–2.

Pontmartin, Armand de, 'Les Historiens de l'illuminisme', in *Causeries littéraires* (Paris, Michel Lévy, 1854), 185–96.[3]

Charles Monselet also refers at length to just one of the studies, that on Rétif, in his own *Rétif de la Bretonne*, first published in 1854.

[1] The date of this review is given by Milner as 25 Dec. 1852, but this could be due to the fact that the Bibliothèque Nationale copy is bound with the 25 Dec. issue at the head. Using the index, it is quite clear that the review is from 10 July, the date of the first issue in vol. 2, and this is verifiable from the accompanying theatre reviews.

[2] Given in *NPl 2* erroneously as 20 March (*NPl 2*, 1710).

[3] Reproduced in its entirety by Henri Bachelin in the Bernouard edition of *Les Illuminés* (1929), 411–19.

Appendix 4: Jules de Prémaray's Review

(This is the full text of the contemporary review of *Les Illuminés* written by Jules de Prémaray, and published on page 4 of *La Patrie*, Tuesday 6 July 1852.)

M. Gérard de Nerval vient de publier un très curieux livre, intitulé: *Les Illuminés, ou les Précurseurs du socialisme*. Je regrette vivement que le grand nombre de volumes qui attendent sur mon bureau m'empêche de consacrer un article entier à l'ouvrage de M. Gérard de Nerval. L'auteur des *Illuminés* est connu de tous. C'est un de ces fins conteurs, de ces savans chercheurs, de ces rares artistes qui font la lumière avec autant de modestie que certains écrivains mettent d'orgueil à faire l'ombre.

On l'aime pour ce qu'il sait, pour ce qu'il pense, pour ce qu'il dit et pour sa manière originale de dire. Eminemment poète, M. Gérard de Nerval voit les choses par leur vrai côté, mais dans le vrai il choisit le grand.

'Il n'est pas donné à tout le monde, dit M. Gérard de Nerval, dans un avant-propos, d'écrire l'*Eloge de la Folie*; mais sans être Erasme,—ou Saint-Evremond, on peut prendre plaisir à tirer du fouillis des siècles quelque figure singulière qu'on s'efforcera de rhabiller ingénieusement,—à restaurer de vieilles toiles, dont la composition bizarre et la peinture éraillée font sourire le vulgaire.[1]—Dans ce temps-ci, où les portraits littéraires ont quelque succès, j'ai voulu peindre certains *excentriques* de la philosophie.'

Ce que M. Gérard de Nerval a tenté, il l'a merveilleusement réussi.

Le Roi de Bicêtre (Raoul Spifame), l'*Histoire de l'abbé de Buquoy* [sic], les *Confidences de Nicolas* (Restif de la Bretonne), *Jacques Cazotte* [,] *Cagliostro* et *Quintus Aucler* sont autant d'études savantes et remplies de faits nouveaux. C'est, suivant l'expression de M. Gérard de Nerval lui-même, l'analyse des bigarrures de l'âme humaine, c'est de la physiologie morale; aussi les *Illuminés* excitent-ils une grande curiosité dans le monde lisant. C'est un des livres les plus recherchés, et, chose rare, le succès de ce livre est complètement justifié par son mérite.

[1] Nerval's text reads: 'font sourire l'amateur vulgaire' (*NPl 2*, 885).

SELECT BIBLIOGRAPHY

❖

This includes only material to which reference is made in the text, and is simply divided into editions of Nerval's works, including those of *Les Illuminés* in order of publication, and other books and articles including works of reference. To the items below may be added the source texts and the different published versions of the individual *récits* detailed in the Appendices: those materials are not repeated here.

I. Works by Nerval

NERVAL, GÉRARD DE, *Les Illuminés* (Paris: Victor Lecou, 1852).

—— *Les Illuminés—Les Faux Saulniers*, vol. iv (1868) of *Œuvres complètes*, Collection Bibliothèque contemporaine, 6 vols. (Paris: Michel Lévy frères, 1867–77).

—— *Les Illuminés*, preface by Henry Frichet, Pages retrouvées, 2 vols. (Paris: André Delpeuch, 1926–7). (Vol. i: 'Les Confidences de Nicolas', vol. ii: 'Cazotte', 'Cagliostro', 'Quintus Aucler', 'Le Roi de Bicêtre'.)

—— *Les Illuminés: récits et portraits*, vol. vi (1927) of [*Œuvres*], introduced and ed. Henri Clouard (Paris: Le Divan, 1927–8).

—— *Les Illuminés*, ed. Aristide Marie (Paris: Champion, 1929).

—— *Les Illuminés*, vol. v (1929) of *Œuvres complètes*, ed. Henri Bachelin, 9 vols. (Paris: François Bernouard, 1927–30).

—— *Les Illuminés*, in vol. iii (1958 (1959)) of *Œuvres*, ed. M. Cornand, 7 vols. (Paris: Imprimerie nationale, Nouvelle Librairie de France, 1958–60).

—— *Les Illuminés*, ed. Robert Kanters (Paris: Nouvel office de l'édition, 1964).

—— *Les Illuminés: le livre des génies fous*, ed. Jean-Baptiste Baronian, Collection Univers secrets (Verviers, Belgium: Bibliothèque Marabout, 1973).

—— *Les Illuminés*, ed. Max Milner (Paris: Gallimard (Folio), 1976).

—— *Les Illuminés: ou les précurseurs du socialisme* (Monaco: Editions du Rocher, 1992).

—— *Œuvres*, ed. Albert Béguin and Jean Richer, Bibliothèque de la Pléiade, 2 vols. (Paris: Gallimard, 1st edn. 1952–6 (*Ancienne Pléiade*); 2nd edn. 1960–6). (Note: references have been simplified into two 'editions', but in fact there are four of vol. i (1952, 1955, then 1960, 1966) for the two of vol. ii (1956, 1960). References are to the later of each pair for vol. i. The second edition (referred to in text where differences require comment) and subsequent editions vary in the numbering of pages and of correspondence.)

—— *Œuvres complètes*, ed. Henri Lemaître, 2 vols. (Paris: Garnier, 1958).

—— *Œuvres complètes*, ed. Jean Guillaume and Claude Pichois, Bibliothèque de la Pléiade, 3 vols. (Paris: Gallimard, 1984–93) (*Nouvelle Pléiade*). (Vol. i: 1989; vol. ii: 1984; vol. iii: 1993).

II. Works of Criticism

ABRAMS, M. H., *Glossary of Literary Terms*, 4th edn. (New York: Rinehart and Winston, 1981; first published 1941).

AMBRIÈRE, MADELEINE (ed.), *Précis de littérature française du XIXe siècle* (Paris: PUF, 1990).

AVNI, ORA, 'A Bicêtre: Austin, Searle, Nerval', *Modern Language Notes* 98 (1983), 4, 624–38.

BARBIER, A.-A., *Dictionnaire des ouvrages anonymes*, 3rd edn., 4 vols. (Paris: Paul Daffis, 1872–9; photographic reprint, Paris: Maisonneuve et Larose, 1964).

BINDER, RAYMOND KIRKMAN, '*Restif de la Bretonne* and *Cazotte*: Two Biographies from *Les Illuminés* by Nerval translated into English' (unpublished doctoral dissertation, University of Iowa, 1976). Summary in *Dissertations Abstracts International* 37 (1976), 5, 2847A.

BLANCHOT, MAURICE, 'Restif de la Bretonne', in *Sade et Restif de la Bretonne* (Brussels: Editions Complexe, 1986), 103–56.

BONNAT, J. L., 'Gérard de Nerval: Lecteur et biographe de Nicolas Restif de la Bretonne. Essai sur les modalités de l'auto-analyse et de son élaboration, à travers biographie et autobiographie, du point de vue du *genre* littéraire' (unpublished monograph, Department of Psychology, University of Nantes, 1980). Includes 'document annexe' by H. Girard, 78–130.

BONNET, HENRI, review of Gérald Schaeffer (*Une Double Lecture*), *Revue d'histoire littéraire de la France* 80 (1980), 1, 130–1.

BONY, JACQUES, *Le Récit nervalien: une recherche des formes* (Paris: Corti, 1990).

—— *L'Esthétique de Nerval* (Paris: SEDES, 1997).

BORGES, JORGE LUIS, 'The Library of Babel', in *Ficciones*, trans. Anthony Kerrigan (London: Weidenfeld and Nicolson, 1962; first published in Spanish 1956).

BOUILLIER, HENRY, 'Gérard et Nicolas', *Cahiers Gérard de Nerval* 12 (1989), 29–37.

BOWMAN, FRANK PAUL, *Gérard de Nerval: la conquête de soi par l'écriture* (Orléans: Paradigme, 1997).

BRIX, MICHEL, 'Nerval journaliste', *Etudes nervaliennes et romantiques* 8 (1986).

—— '*Les Illuminés* de Nerval, ou le "livre parfaitement sensé sur des folies"', *Studi Francesi* 102 (1990), 464–71.

—— 'Nerval, *Les Illuminés* et le scepticisme', *Romanische Forschungen* 106 (1994), 1–4, 243–53.

—— 'Manuel bibliographique des œuvres de Gérard de Nerval', *Etudes nervaliennes et romantiques* 11 (1997), 1–506.

BROMBERT, VICTOR, *La Prison romantique: essai sur l'imaginaire* (Paris: Corti, 1975).

BRUNET, GUSTAVE, *Dictionnaire des ouvrages anonymes suivi des Supercheries littéraires dévoilées. Supplément* [...], (Paris: F.-J. Féchoz, 1889; photographic reprint Paris: Maisonneuve et Larose, 1964).

—— *Les Fous littéraires: essai bibliographique sur la littérature excentrique, les illuminés, visionnaires etc.* (Brussels, 1880; reprinted Geneva: Slatkine, 1970).

CASSAGNAU, ROBERT, 'Gérard de Nerval bibliophile et les bibliothécaires', *Revue française d'Histoire du Livre* 41 (1983), 367–81.

CASTILLO, DEBRA A., *The Translated World: A Postmodern Tour of Libraries in Literature* (Tallahassee: Florida State University Press [1984]).

CAWS, MARY ANN (ed.), *City Images: Perspectives from Literature, Philosophy and Film* (New York: Gordon and Breach, 1991).

CÉARD, JEAN, 'Raoul Spifame, Roi de Bicêtre: recherches sur un récit de Nerval', *Etudes nervaliennes et romantiques* 3 (1981), 25–50.

CELLIER, LÉON, 'Où en sont les recherches sur Gérard de Nerval?', *Archives des Lettres modernes* 3 (1957), 1–32.

CHAINTREAU, ANNE-MARIE, and LEMAÎTRE, RENÉE, *Drôles de bibliothèques: Le Thème de la bibliothèque dans la littérature et le cinéma* (Paris: Editions du Cercle de la Librairie, 1990).

CHAMBERS, ROSS, *Gérard de Nerval et la poétique du voyage* (Paris: Corti, 1969).

—— 'Récits d'aliénés, récits aliénés: Nerval et John Perceval', *Poétique* 53 (1983), 72–90.

CHAMPFLEURY (pseud. of JULES HUSSON), *Les Excentriques* (Paris: Michel Lévy, 1852).

—— *Grandes Figures d'hier et d'aujourd'hui,* Œuvres illustrées de Champfleury (Paris: Poulet-Malassis et de Broise, 1861).

CHASLES, PHILARÈTE, 'Les Excentriques', *Revue des Deux Mondes* (1 September 1834), 497–558.

DÉCOTE, GEORGES, 'Irrationalisme et illuminisme au dix-huitième siècle: Notes bibliographiques', *Le Français dans le monde* 49 (1967), 6–11.

DESTRUEL, PHILIPPE, '*Angélique* et la Bibliothèque de Babel', *Romantisme* 48 (1985), 21–32.

Dictionnaire de l'Académie (7th edn. 1878).

DIDIER, BÉATRICE, 'Révolution et identité dans *Les Illuminés*', *Cahiers Gérard de Nerval* 12 (1989), 2–10.

DUNN, SUSAN, 'Nerval, Transgression and the Amendement Riancey', *Nineteenth-Century French Studies* 12 (1983–4), 86–95.

DUPRÉ, GUY, 'Les Illuminés ou les précurseurs du socialisme', *L'Infini* 38 (1992), 94–115.

ECO, UMBERTO, *The Name of the Rose*, trans. William Weaver (London: Martin Secker and Warburg, 1983; first published in Italian 1980).

EDWARDS, PETER J., 'Problèmes d'études de manuscrits: le cas de Nerval', in *Sur la génétique textuelle*, ed. D. G. Bevan and P. M. Wetherill (Amsterdam: Rodopi, 1990), 55–63.

ELIOT, T. S., *The Sacred Wood: Essays on Poetry and Criticism* (London: Methuen, 1920).

ENCKELL, PIERRE, 'Et vous pensiez connaître Nerval?', *L'Evénement du jeudi* (30 November 1989), 134.

FELMAN, SHOSHANA, *La Folie et la chose littéraire* (Paris: Seuil, 1978).

FOUCAULT, MICHEL, *Folie et déraison: histoire de la folie à l'âge classique* (Paris: Plon, 1961).

—— 'Un "Fantastique" de la bibliothèque', *Cahiers Renaud-Barrault* 59 (1967), 7–30. Reprinted as 'La Bibliothèque fantastique' in Gérard Genette and Tzvetan Todorov (eds.), *Travail de Flaubert* (Paris: Seuil, 1983), 103–22.

FURST, LILIAN R., *Fictions of Romantic Irony in European Narrative 1760–1857* (London: Macmillan, 1984).

GASCAR, PIERRE, *Gérard de Nerval et son temps* (Paris: Gallimard, 1981).

GAUCHERON, JACQUES, review of Gérald Schaeffer (*Une Double Lecture*), *Europe* 604–5 (1979), 243–4.

GAUKROGER, STEPHEN, *Descartes: An Intellectual Biography* (Oxford: Clarendon Press, 1995).

GAUTIER, THÉOPHILE, *Les Grotesques* (Fasano and Paris: Schana/Nizet, 1985; first published Paris: Desessart 1844).

GENETTE, GÉRARD, *Seuils* (Paris: Seuil, 1987).

GENINASCA, JACQUES, *Analyse structurale des 'Chimères' de Nerval* (Neuchâtel: La Baconnière, 1971).

GILBERT, CLAIRE, *Nerval's Double: A Structural Study* (University, Mississippi: Romance Monographs Inc., 1979).

GIRARD, H., *see* BONNAT.

GIRARDIN, EMILE DE, *La Politique universelle: décrets de l'avenir* (Brussels: C. Muquart, 1852).

GODEFROY, FRÉDÉRIC, *Dictionnaire de l'ancienne langue française (IXe au XVe siècles)* 10 vols. (Paris: Vieweg, 1881–1902).

GUILLAUME, JEAN, and PICHOIS, CLAUDE, 'Chronologie de sa vie et de son œuvre, août 1850–juin 1852', *Etudes nervaliennes et romantiques* 6 (1984).

D'HAUTEFEUILLE, MME, [HAUTEFEUILLE, ANNE DE BEAUREPAIRE, ÉPOUSE TEXIER D'] 'La Famille Cazotte', in *Le Correspondant* (1845), published as one volume the following year under the pseudonym Anna-Marie.

JATON, ANNE-MARIE, 'Nerval "historien" des Illuminés', in *Lumières et Illuminisme: actes du colloque international de Cortona* (October 1983), ed. Mario Matucci (Pisa: Pacini Editore, 1984), 29–40.

JEAN, RAYMOND, *Nerval par lui-même*, Collection Ecrivains de Toujours (Paris: Seuil, 1964).

JEANNERET, MICHEL, 'Nerval et la biographie impossible', *French Studies* 24 (1970), 127–43.

—— *La Lettre perdue: écriture et folie dans l'œuvre de Nerval* (Paris: Flammarion, 1978).

JONES, R. E., *Gérard de Nerval* (New York: Twayne, 1976).

KASELL, WALTER, 'Nerval's Innocent Double: "Le Roi de Bicêtre"', *Stanford French Review* 2 (1978), 1, 39–46.

KOFMAN, SARAH, *Nerval: le charme de la répétition* (Lausanne: L'Age d'homme, 1979).

LATOURNERIE, JACQUES, '*Les Illuminés*: Gérard de Nerval et Umberto Eco', *Cahiers Gérard de Nerval* 14 (1991), 83–6.

LEJEUNE, PHILIPPE, *Je est un autre: l'autobiographie de la littérature aux médias* (Paris: Seuil, 1980).

LOKKE, KARI, *Gérard de Nerval: The Poet as Social Visionary* (Lexington, Kentucky: French Forum, 1987).

MARIE, ARISTIDE, *Bibliographie des œuvres de Nerval* (Paris: Champion, 1926).

MARSAN, JULES (ed.), *Gérard de Nerval: Correspondance (1830–1855)* (Paris: Mercure de France, 1911).

MATUCCI, MARIO, *see* JATON.

MILNER, MAX, and PICHOIS, CLAUDE, *Littérature française, VII: De Chateaubriand à Baudelaire* (Paris: Arthaud, 1985; rev. edn. 1990).

MONSELET, CHARLES, *Oubliés et Dédaignés: Linguet, Fréron, Rétif de la Bretonne, Mercier, Cubières* (Paris: Bachelin-Deflorenne, 1885).

MOUILLAUD, GENEVIÈVE, 'L'Auteur et l'autre', *L'Herne* 37 (1980), 243–56.

MURAY, PHILIPPE, *Le Dix-neuvième Siècle à travers les âges* (Paris: Denoël, 1984).

NODIER, CHARLES, *Histoire du roi de Bohême et de ses sept châteaux* (Paris: Delangle, 1830; reprinted Paris: Plasma, 1979).

—— *Bibliographie des fous: de quelques livres excentriques* (Paris: Techener, 1835).

PAULY, REBECCA M., *Le Berceau et la bibliothèque: le paradoxe de l'écriture autobiographique*, Stanford French and Italian Studies 62 (Saratoga: Anma Libri, 1989).

PONTMARTIN, ARMAND DE, *Causeries littéraires* (Paris: Michel Lévy frères, 1854).

PRENDERGAST, CHRISTOPHER, *The Order of Mimesis: Balzac, Stendhal, Nerval, Flaubert* (Cambridge: Cambridge University Press, 1986).

RÉTIF DE LA BRETONNE, NICOLAS, *Monsieur Nicolas, ou le cœur humain dévoilé*, ed. Pierre Testud, Bibliothèque de la Pléiade (Paris: Gallimard, 1989).

RICHER, JEAN, *Gérard de Nerval et les doctrines ésotériques* (Paris: Griffon d'or, 1947).

—— *Nerval: Expérience et création* (Paris: Hachette, 1963; rev. edn. 1970).

RINSLER, NORMA, 'Gérard de Nerval and Heinrich Heine', *Revue de littérature comparée* 33 (1959), 1, 94–102.

—— review of Gérald Schaeffer (*Une Double Lecture*), *French Studies* 34 (1980), 88.

ROUSSEL, JEAN, 'De Girardin à Nerval: la célébrité des soupers d'Ermenonville', *Œuvres et critiques* 10 (1985), 1, 7–18.

SANGSUE, DANIEL, 'Propositions pour une lecture d'*Angélique*', *Lendemains* 33 (1984), 21–30.

—— *Le Récit excentrique: Gautier, De Maistre, Nerval, Nodier* (Paris: Corti, 1987).

—— 'Démesures du livre', *Romantisme* 69 (1990), 43–59.

SCHAEFFER, GÉRALD, *Une Double Lecture de Gérard de Nerval*: '*Les Illuminés*' *et* '*Les Filles du Feu*', Collection Langages (Neuchâtel: Baconnière/Payot, 1977).

SCHÄRER, KURT, *Thématique de Nerval ou le monde recomposé* (Paris: Minard, 1968).

SENELIER, JEAN, *Gérard de Nerval : Essai de bibliographie* (Paris: Nizet, 1959).

—— *Bibliographie nervalienne 1960–67* (Paris: Nizet, 1968).

—— *Bibliographie nervalienne 1968–80* (Paris: Nizet, 1982).

—— *Bibliographie nervalienne 1981–89* (Paris: Nizet, 1991).

SIMON, GUSTAVE, *Histoire d'une collaboration: Alexandre Dumas et Auguste Maquet* (Paris: Crès, 1919).

STREIFF MORETTI, MONIQUE, 'Portraits dans une bibliothèque: Nerval, Töpffer et quelques autres', *Cahiers Gérard de Nerval* 5 (1982), 23–36.

TESTUD, PIERRE, *Rétif de la Bretonne et la création littéraire* (Geneva: Droz, 1977).

TÖPFFER, RODOLPHE, *La Bibliothèque de mon oncle* (Geneva: Imprimerie de la Bibliothèque universelle, 1832).

TRITSMANS, BRUNO, *Ecritures nervaliennes* (Tübingen: Gunter Narr, 1993).

TYERS, MERYL, '"Worth half a dozen novels": Une critique des *Illuminés* de Nerval dans *The Westminster Review*', *Cahiers Gérard de Nerval* 15 (1992), 94–6.

—— 'Un Compte-rendu des *Illuminés* dans *La Patrie*', *French Studies Bulletin* 46 (1993), 9–11.

VIATTE, AUGUSTE, *Les Sources occultes du romantisme: Illuminisme—Théosophie, 1770–1820*, 2 vols. (Paris: Champion, 1928).

VILLAS, JAMES, *Gérard de Nerval: A Critical Bibliography 1900–1967* (Columbia, Missouri: University of Missouri Press, 1968).

VILLIERS DE L'ISLE-ADAM, J. M. M. P. A., comte de, *Contes cruels* (Paris: Garnier, 1968; first published Paris: Calmann-Lévy, 1883).

WARTBURG, WALTHER VON, *Französisches Etymologisches Wörterbuch*, 14 vols. (various towns and publishers, 1928–61).

Wellesley Index to Victorian Periodicals 1824–1900, ed. Walter E. Houghton, 5 vols. (Toronto and Buffalo: University of Toronto Press, 1979).

ZIMMERMANN, MARTIN, 'La Bibliothèque de l'oncle: un motif et ses significations', *Cahiers Gérard de Nerval* 14 (1991), 55–62.

ZINK, MICHEL, 'Nerval in the Library, or the Archives of the Soul', *Representations* 56 (1996), 96–105.

ZUCKERMAN, PHYLLIS, 'History, Fiction and Legend in Nerval's *Angélique*', *Sub-Stance* 20 (1978), 79–90.

INDEX